✔ **W9-DAW-764**

640 Bay Road
Queensbury, NY 12804

DISCARDED

HADRIAN'S WALL
AND ITS PEOPLE

This is the first book to provide a picture of how the Wall functioned on a day-to-day basis, and of the impact it had on ordinary people, be they soldiers or native Britons. Moving beyond questions of military organisation and construction techniques, military life is instead discussed in terms of the experiences of the ordinary soldier and his family. Civilian life is also considered in some detail – including the way close contact with the army influenced civilian life in the north of Britain and the contentious issue of 'Romanisation'.

Geraint Osborn uses archaeological evidence and the content of the Vindolanda tablets – a remarkable collection of wooden writing tablets found at the fort of the same name – to give a rounded picture of life along the Wall. He also explores what happened to Christian communities of the Wall area after the Roman army's departure. Finally he assesses the ideological role which the Wall played in the nineteenth century, as British imperial identity came to rely upon the Roman empire as model and justification.

The book includes tips on places to visit, a guide to further reading and a handy combined index and glossary.

Geraint Osborn has taught Ancient History in the Universities of Bristol, Cardiff and Durham. His main interests are Roman Britain and Gaul and the history of the later Roman empire.

GREECE & ROME LIVE

Also available in this series:
Ancient Greece in Film and Popular Culture, Gideon Nisbet (2006)
Augustine: The Confessions, Gillian Clark (2004)
Gruesome Deaths and Celibate Lives: Christian Martyrs and Ascetics, Aideen Hartney (2005)
Julius Caesar, Robert Garland (2004)

Forthcoming titles:
After Virgil: The Poetry, Politics and Perversion of Roman Epic, Robert Cowan
Ancient Rome at the Cinema: Story and Spectacle in Hollywood and Rome, Elena Theodorakopoulos
Augustus: Caesar's Web: Power & Propaganda in Augustan Rome, Matthew D.H. Clark
The Classical Greek House, Janett Morgan
Greek Tyranny, Sian Lewis
Hannibal: Rome's Greatest Enemy, Dexter Hoyos
The Law in Ancient Greece, Christopher Carey
Pausanias: An Ancient Guide to Greece, John Taylor
The Plays of Sophocles, James Morwood
The Politics of Greek Tragedy, David M. Carter
Reading Catullus, John Godwin
The Trojan War, Emma Stafford

HADRIAN'S WALL AND ITS PEOPLE

Geraint Osborn

BRISTOL
PHOENIX
PRESS

Cover illustration: William Bell Scott, *The Building of a Roman Wall*
(Wallington, The Trevelyan Collection: The National Trust/NTPL/Derrick E. Witty)

First published in 2006 by
Bristol Phoenix Press
an imprint of The Exeter Press
Reed Hall, Streatham Drive,
Exeter, Devon, EX4 4QR
UK

www.exeterpress.co.uk

© Geraint Osborn 2006

The right of Geraint Osborn to be identified
as author of this work has been asserted by him
in accordance with the Copyright, Designs and
Patents Act 1988.

British Library Cataloguing in Publication Data
A catalogue record for this book is available
from the British Library.

ISBN-10: 1-904675-19-0 (Paperback)
ISBN-13: 978-1-904675-19-8 (Paperback)

ISBN-10: 1-904675-44-1 (Hardback)
ISBN-13: 978-1-904675-44-0 (Hardback)

Printed in Great Britain by
Antony Rowe Limited, Chippenham

In loving memory of my grandfathers,
John Osborn
and
Canon Philip Hobbs MBE

Contents

Illustrations

Preface and acknowledgements

Many volumes have been written on Hadrian's Wall, ranging from weighty academic tomes to beautifully illustrated children's books. My aim in adding to this body of work is two-fold. In the first place, being a social (as opposed to a military or political) historian, I seek to offer a picture of ordinary people – soldiers, farmers, merchants and others – who lived in and close to the forts of the Wall. After giving a brief history of the Wall and its study in ch. 1, I go on to ask why so grand a monument was built in the north of Roman Britain (ch. 2); I examine the lives of soldiers and their impact on, and role in, the region (ch. 3); I look at the local farmers and the often foreign merchants of the civilian settlements (ch. 4); I analyse the ways in which life changed when the military presence was withdrawn from Britain in the early fifth century (ch. 5); and I point out finally that a social history of Hadrian's Wall is more difficult to write than a military one because of deep-seated nineteenth-century (mis)conceptions of the role of the Roman army in Britain (ch. 6).

In the second place I wish to show how historians and archaeologists analyse evidence, deal with its problems and reach conclusions. History has deservedly in recent years become very popular on television but all too often the viewer is presented with firm answers, supported by sound-bites from noted experts; a sense of how history works is frequently missing. In discussing the people whose lives revolved around Hadrian's Wall I have tried to begin with analysis of the often fragmentary evidence, so that the readers may see for themselves how I have come to my conclusions.

To avoid confusion later, the issue of place-names should be dealt with at the outset. The names by which we designate the sites along Hadrian's Wall and in the rest of Roman Britain are not those used in the Roman period; Saxon, Viking and Norman interventions in the country have since had an enormous effect on the English language and on place-names. For the convenience of those who may know Hadrian's Wall already or may intend to visit the area, I have throughout used modern English place-names instead of their Latin equivalents – Cirencester rather than *Corinium*, York rather than *Eboracum*, London rather than *Londinium* – when talking about Britain in general; and along Hadrian's Wall, for instance, Carlisle rather than *Luguvallium*, Birdoswald rather than *Banna*, Wallsend rather than *Segedunum*. There are two exceptions: in the south I have chosen to use *Verulamium* in place of St Albans, because the modern town does not lie precisely over the Roman town (as modern Cirencester, for instance, does over Roman *Corinium*); and in the region of the Wall I have regularly used Latin *Vindolanda* in discussion of the fort at Chesterholm. This second anomaly is for the benefit of readers: *Vindolanda* is by far the more common usage both in books on the Wall and, more importantly, on road-signs in the area.

In writing this book I have benefited enormously from the advice and encouragement of a number of people. Without the love and patience of my wife Julia, it would never have been completed; I am also most grateful to her for encouraging me to see the veterinary and medical aspects of life on Hadrian's Wall and providing me with expert advice (as did Roisin McInery and Eric Morgan) on those topics. I would also like to thank my parents, who first took me to Hadrian's Wall as an infant and have continued to encourage my ancient historical interests ever since. William, Charlotte and Philippa deserve thanks, not least for their patience as children, when cries of 'not another Roman site' accompanied our visits. Jo Kear has shown me how interesting and important nineteenth- and twentieth-century uses of Rome could be and thus inspired my final chapter; while Neville Morley, Richard Brickstock and Richard Hingley have all been unstinting in their advice and encouragement; I am particularly grateful to Richard Hingley for providing me with a copy of his article on rural settlement. The contribution of John Betts as editor should also be mentioned; his encouragement and understanding of a first-time author have made writing this book much more enjoyable and less stressful than it might have been. Lastly, but by no means least, my thanks go to those who have read drafts of this book: Julia Osborn, Nicky and Nigel Osborn, Meryl Key, Tony Sarma, and Daniela Bowker.

Roman Britain

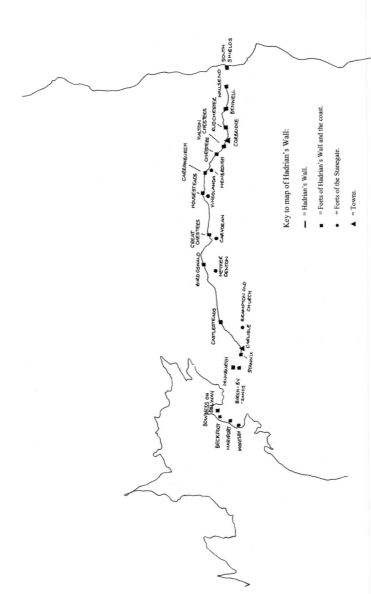

Key to map of Hadrian's Wall:

————— = Hadrian's Wall.

◼ = Forts of Hadrian's Wall and the coast.

● = Forts of the Stanegate.

▲ = Towns.

Hadrian's Wall

Chapter 1

Introduction

As the A1 circles to the west of Newcastle, you can turn westward onto the A69 and almost immediately come upon a short length of ancient stonework, marked – for the observant car passenger – as 'Hadrian's Wall'. A few miles further on the A69 swings away southward; and there a slightly complicated turn will take you onto the B6318. This road, as it wends its way towards Carlisle takes driver, cyclist or walker past – occasionally even over – constant reminders of the region's Roman past. At times lengths of Roman wall or deep ditches can be seen to right or left; in a few places along the road between the forts of Chesters and Carrawburgh the two come together, so that as the car reaches the top of a hill, the remains of the Roman landscape are laid out perfectly below. Wall, ditch and *vallum* (the structure running south of the wall – see pp. 7 and 24-7 below), are each to be clearly seen. The military remains are obvious; for those of us who read as children the books of Rosemary Sutcliffe, of Kipling or Marshall's *Our Island Story*, they evoke images of red-crested Roman legionaries. Yet what lies before the driver as he descends the hill is only one part of the complex military and social structure which shaped this area between the first and the fifth centuries AD. This was a frontier, manned by Roman soldiers – or at least by soldiers from all over the Roman empire who fought in the name of the Roman emperor. It was also home to local farmers and tradesmen, even to foreign merchants, their lives revolving around those soldiers, whose presence had an enormous impact upon northern British economy and society. This book aims to examine all of these people, who between them made the society of Britain's northern frontier so distinctive.

The background to Hadrian's Wall

The Romans first came to Britain under the general Julius Caesar, who fought two campaigns in the south in 55 and 54 BC. His motives for coming to Britain in the first place have been hotly debated by historians in arguments that need not be rehearsed here; suffice to say that Caesar's campaigns brought Britain, if not immediately into the Roman empire, then at least within the ambit of Roman territorial designs. Nearly a hundred years were to pass before the emperor Claudius – a character no doubt familiar to older readers from the BBC dramatisation of Robert Graves' *I, Claudius* and *Claudius the God* – brought the legions once again to Britain in AD 43. Claudius cannot have expected to become emperor but, in the political turmoil following the death of his predecessor Caligula, he was elevated to the position of emperor by the Praetorian Guard, the elite troops of the Roman army. He was a grandson of Augustus, Rome's first emperor, and in fact uncle to Caligula; but a weak constitution and serious illness throughout his life meant that he had always been regarded as a minor, ineffectual member of the imperial family, not a possible successor. Doubtless the Praetorian Guard saw him as their puppet to be manipulated. The result was that, to survive the political machinations of a Roman senate which still recalled the days before Augustus, when it ruled Rome as a republic, Claudius needed military success. Roman ideology said that military victories and the expansion of empire were vital; to survive as emperor by achieving military victory, Claudius picked on Britain.[1]

In the gradual development of Roman rule in Britain, the north did not fall under direct Roman control before the 70s AD. The governors of Britain at that time, controlling the province for the emperor Vespasian (who had himself earlier fought in the conquest of the west-country), pushed gradually north; by AD 79 the third of these governors, Julius Agricola, had penetrated far into Scotland, leaving conquered tribes behind him under Roman control and reaching the river Tay. His campaigns were recorded in detail by his son-in-law, the historian Tacitus, whose *Agricola* provides an account of the Romanisation of Britain. In AD 79 Vespasian died; Agricola's advance was halted until AD 82 in the reign of

Domitian, when he and his armies once again moved north. The end result was the battle of Mons Graupius in 83, at which the Scottish tribes were defeated; but the victory was not pursued. Instead, Agricola, having served far longer than was usual for a governor of Britain, was recalled to Rome. At much the same time a crisis on the Danube frontier seems to have meant that one of the four legions of Britain, the *II Adiutrix*, was also withdrawn from Britain. Loss of the experienced governor and commander combined with withdrawl of a legion meant that, whereas the Roman army had held all Britain at least as far as a line between the estuaries of Forth and Clyde, by the end of the first century AD it had withdrawn to hold a line further south between Tyne and Solway.

There is debate about the precise date of the Roman withdrawal from Scotland to the Tyne-Solway isthmus. Archaeology rarely allows exactly precise dating and our literary sources for the period concentrate on events closer to Rome. The evidence from finds of Roman coins suggests that the area north of the Forth-Clyde line was abandoned in the mid-80s, when the army consolidated its position there. After that, however, we largely have a blank; forts north of the Tyne-Solway line were abandoned in an orderly fashion, their wooden structures burnt; but we cannot be sure whether this happened under Domitian (AD 81-96), Nerva (96-98) or Trajan (98-117).

Since the withdrawal from Scotland created the frontier which Hadrian's Wall would mark, it is worth spending a little time over this problem. On the one hand, it seems unlikely that Trajan could be responsible; he was extremely ambitious for the glory of military success, putting much effort into expansion of the empire's boundaries through his Dacian and Parthian wars. It is hard to picture him actively choosing at the same time to give up territory in Britain. This argument suggests that responsibility for the withdrawal may have lain with Domitian or Nerva. We tend, however, to judge the question from a British perspective, which magnifies her importance. The island had, of course, offered relatively easy military glory to Julius Caesar and to Claudius but it was not a significant part of the empire, unless an emperor specifically chose to draw attention to it. A British rebellion might draw such attention, casting a shadow over Trajan's successes elsewhere; so we may speculate that a quiet withdrawal from Scotland meant that Britain would be easier to hold with three, rather than the previous four, legions. Trajan could then concentrate on his eastern wars without distraction. The situation might be seen as one in which Britain offered little chance for further glory, though plenty of opportunity for embarrassment if mismanaged. At the same time it is hard to see Domitian making a decision to halt further expansion into Scotland and to consolidate a position in southern Scotland, then ordering a withdrawal. He continued campaigning in the east but, arguably, with the aim of strengthening existing frontiers and dealing with troublesome kings on Rome's borders. A decision to hold Scotland south of the Forth-Clyde isthmus would match his aims elsewhere. Nerva is an equally unlikely candidate for the decision to withdraw to the Tyne-Solway line. He reigned for just sixteen months – a period racked with problems which stemmed, in large measure, from his difficulties with the troops; the statesman and letter-writer Pliny the Younger reports unrest among the frontier armies. To make major changes to the frontiers of empire at such a time would seem an unwise – and thus unlikely – move.

Whenever the move took place, the southward withdrawal meant that Trajan was eventually holding what appears to have been an earlier frontier between Tyne and Solway. A road ran between the two forts of Carlisle in the west and Corbridge in the east, generally known to historians by its mediaeval name, the Stanegate. Along its line lie several other forts – in order east from Corbridge to the west, Newbrough, Vindolanda, Carvoran, Nether Denton and Brampton Old Church, ending at Carlisle. Corbridge, Vindolanda, Nether Denton and Carlisle can each be dated as early as AD 69-96 (during the time of the Flavian emperors, Vespasian, Titus and Domitian); the other Stanegate forts have produced evidence only from later periods, though it has to be said that they have hardly been comprehensively excavated. It is hard to see this cohesive line of forts post-dating Hadrian, since the presence of the wall would almost certainly render other forts a couple of miles to the south redundant. Yet on the original scheme for the wall, the only accommodation for soldiers was provided in the milecastles; there were no forts on the wall itself. This only serves to reinforce the theory that plenty of forts must have existed along the Stanegate already; it is inconceivable that the wall would have been built with no thought of housing the soldiers who must man it.[2]

The wall itself, then, at first complemented the Stanegate and then rendered it largely irrelevant, although the Stanegate forts continued to operate. It was the brainchild of the emperor Hadrian, who visited Britain in AD 121 as part of a tour of all of the provinces of the empire. The wall was begun in 122 and originally constructed partly in stone – from Newcastle to the river Irthing (45 Roman miles) – and partly in turf – from the Irthing to the Solway (31 Roman miles). The use of turf suggests that resources of stone in the western sector were less easily accessible. Towards the end of Hadrian's reign, in the mid- to late 130s, the turf section was eventually replaced in stone; the wall was also extended at its eastern end from Newcastle to Wallsend. Milecastles, with

Fig.1 The North gate of Milecastle 37, just west of Housesteads fort

interior measurements of roughly fifteen metres square were placed, as their name suggests, at every Roman mile (fig. 1). Good examples can be seen at Harrow's Scar and Poltross Burn, close to Birdoswald, as well as just west of Housesteads. They contained one or two small buildings which it is reasonable to assume were barracks for the soldiers stationed there; doubtless, after a period of duty, the soldiers would return to the forts on the Stanegate to be replaced by others. The milecastles served as lookout points; the fact that they were positioned at gates in the wall demonstrates that they also regulated passage across the frontier. For the wall was not a closed frontier like the present fence running along the West Bank in Israel; rather, it controlled passage from side to side (see pp. 20-22 below) – and the milecastles were crucial in this process. They were augmented by turrets placed every third of a mile, which functioned only as watchtowers. It is impossible to say whether soldiers slept there; or whether they were replaced at frequent intervals by men from the milecastles.

It is from the milecastles that attempts have been made to estimate the height of the wall. The height of the gates at each milecastle suggests that the wall was designed to be fifteen Roman feet (four metres and forty centimetres) high; the gate at Housesteads milecastle, for example, was four metres and sixteen centimetres high. It seems reasonable to suppose that the wall would be higher than the gates but, on the basis of more extensive foundations around milecastle gates, as well as remains of a stairway, it has been suggested that they were surmounted by a tower. This would mean that, in practical terms, the gate could be higher than the wall. In the end, however, there is no way to be certain from foundations alone.

The wall was bounded on either side by ditches. That to the north is not consistently present. In places it was simply not begun (on Cockmount Hill, for example); in others a ditch could simply not be dug. This is particularly true of the sections to the east and west of Housesteads, where the wall runs along the top of a line of hills, effectively on a cliff-edge (fig. 2). Where it exists, the ditch is usually around six metres in front of the wall, doubtless to prevent the weight of the wall collapsing the ditch and thus the wall itself.[3] The width of the ditch varies between eight and twelve metres; it was between two and a half and three metres in depth. Thus, it was a serious impediment to anyone wishing to approach too close to the wall. However the ditch was not primarily a defensive structure, since the wall itself was not essentially defensive (see pp. 20-22 below); its main function was surely to prevent people getting close enough to climb the wall. Its presence must have forced those wishing to cross from north to south or *vice versa* to use the gates which could be approached by a causeway. So the ditch was

Fig. 2 Hadrian's Wall west of Housesteads

a way of enforcing Roman control over movements of the local population. If crossing the frontier was not easy, then the presence of the frontier was much more obvious.

The ditch to the rear of the wall, known as the *vallum*, has attracted much attention (see further ch. 2 below). It was dug just a few years after the wall was begun, at the same time as new forts were built on the line of the wall; such is its size that it would have made moving construction materials onto the site of the wall extremely difficult. At the forts it was crossed by a causeway; otherwise it would have been well-nigh impassable. The *vallum* was a flat-bottomed ditch twenty Roman feet wide and ten deep; on either side, set back thirty Roman feet, lay two mounds, twenty Roman feet wide.[4] The *vallum*'s presence could not be ignored; it is an impressive monument on its own. By the third century, however, it had effectively been abandoned, either made redundant or its significance forgotten; expanding civilian settlements associated with each fort began to straddle it and were even permitted to fill in its ditch and flatten its mounds.

As the *vallum* was being built, so forts were being constructed on the actual line of the wall. This was begun under the governorship of A. Platorius Nepos, who governed the province from AD 122 until at least 124; the next governor known in Britain, L. Trebius Germanus, can be dated only from 127 – so it is possible that Nepos was in charge until that date. Inscriptions from the forts record much of the work as being done under Nepos. A swift decision to change the original design of the wall and incorporate forts along its line had evidently been taken. Since there are more on the wall than on the Stanegate, it may have been decided to increase the number of soldiers stationed in the area. New forts had, therefore, to be built somewhere and having soldiers permanently manning the wall, rather than travelling several miles from the Stanegate forts to go on duty, seems to modern eyes a sensible decision.

In this survey of the building of the wall, its brief abandonment should be mentioned. Hadrian's adopted son, Antoninus Pius, decided to push the frontier north once again. (On the strength of this move his coins are the first regularly to bear the recognisable figure of Britannia.) From the 140s until the 160s Hadrian's Wall ceased to act as the frontier of the empire; that function was taken up by the Antonine Wall, built of turf on a stone foundation, across the Forth-Clyde isthmus. The reasons for this, then for its subsequent abandonment are quite unclear; so are the precise dates. Hadrian's Wall was not, however, completely abandoned in the interim: two inscriptions mark building work on it during the 150s; and sufficient of the wall-forts have evidence of continued occupation in the period to suggest that, even if the wall lost its significance as a frontier, its forts were still manned. Birdoswald, Carlisle, Chesters, Corbridge and Vindolanda all provide evidence of the presence of soldiers in the period; these cover not just one region but the whole length of both the wall and the Stanegate. So it may be argued that the impact of the Antonine Wall on the Tyne-Solway military zone was limited.

Economy and society

Necessary to any analysis of Hadrian's Wall is a brief consideration of the socio-economic context of which it was a part. In other words, the wall should not be viewed – and cannot be properly understood – in isolation from the rest of Roman Britain. For all that it lay at the northernmost extremity of the province *Britannia Inferior*, it was still a part of the whole Romano-British system. It differs from the rest in crucial ways but the significance of those very differences cannot be appreciated unless the entire system is itself understood.

The Roman invasion and occupation of Britain brought with it a new social order, one which had its roots in the Mediterranean and was thus alien to Britain's various peoples. To begin with Britain had been a loose conglomeration of tribes; while we lack written evidence and the certainty that might provide, it seems highly unlikely that they had any sense of themselves as a unified entity. Loyalty can only have been to local tribal chiefs and gods, an iron-age tribesmen seeing himself as one of the Brigantes or the Dobunni, not as a Briton. The Romans' administration, on the other hand, was organised in far larger areas, in provinces (*provinciae*). That they had a sense of Britain as a single entity is reflected in the name of the province. Britain was initially governed as one (*Britannia*) but reorganised in the later second or early-third century as two provinces: *Britannia Inferior* including the area from Hadrian's Wall southward as far as a line running probably from the Mersey to the Wash, governed from the city of York (*Eboracum*): and *Britannia Superior*, covering the area from that line southward, governed from London (*Londinium*).This bipartite arrangement survived until the late third century.[5] The initial effect of the Romans upon Britain, then, was perhaps to create a notion of 'Britain', even if it was one which only occasionally included Scotland or parts of it. However the Roman impact was by no means limited to that.

As the initial and primary means of controlling Britain, the army was a significant presence; four legions of the twenty nine available to the emperors – a total of over twenty one thousand men – were stationed in Britain during the first century AD, together with about thirty-five thousand auxiliary troops. This is a very high concentration of soldiers in one relatively small area; and, even when one legion was withdrawn from Britain towards the end of the first century AD, removing something like five thousand, three hundred men, the total number remained over fifty thousand.[6] None of them, even when stationed in one area for a long time, were involved in agriculture; they did not feed themselves. And, while there is a great deal of evidence for military workshops within forts, no unit was self-sufficient in other areas. Pottery, clothes, armour, building materials – all had to be produced, paid for, then transported to the army wherever it was stationed. The military presence thus had an immediate effect on the economy and infrastructure of Britain. There are many reasons for the great Roman road-building programme in Britain and across the empire. It marked their presence and their dominance over local populations indelibly onto the landscape, replacing former dirt tracks with wide, well-laid, stone-paved highways. It also greatly facilitated the movement of goods, which reached their destination more quickly, thus more cheaply and, in the case of perishable foodstuffs, in better condition.

Economically, the impact of the Roman army on Britain was enormous – a theme which will run throughout this book. Yet it is worth noting that, as Richard Reece has pointed out in his excellent *My Roman Britain*, it was not just the size of the army which had the impact. It is obviously impossible to be quite certain about the population of either Roman or pre-Roman Britain. Only the cities, the towns and a number of the villas are known in any detail; and, while we can be reasonably sure that no urban sites remain to be discovered, we have no idea how many villas lie unknown in the ground. We cannot know what proportion of the total number of villas occupied in Britain have so far been uncovered by archaeologists. We have sufficient remains of villages and farmsteads to be certain that they existed in great numbers throughout the province but their total number remains a mystery. So we cannot completely map the settlements. Even when we know a site well (the cities of Verulamium, Silchester or Wroxeter, for example, which have been comprehensively excavated since they do not lie beneath modern cities), we can still have little idea of how many people lived there. How many people shared a house? We simply do not know. The number will in any case have varied from family to family. Yet Reece has argued that it is possible to produce an approximation of the total population of Roman Britain by other means.

It must be remembered that the majority of the population were farmers. 'Cities' were tiny – by today's standards mere villages rather than cities, deserving their status not so much by virtue of their size but because of the central administrative role they played within society. Each farmer, constrained by a lack of pesticides and modern fertilisers and by an absence of modern farm-machinery, produced only a small surplus; most of what he grew fed him and his family, either directly (his grain made his bread, for example) or because he could exchange produce with his neighbour (the milk from his cows for his neighbour's freshly butchered pork, perhaps). Surplus output, either paid as rent to the farmer's landlord, if he didn't own his own land, or sold to a merchant, effectively allowed the city dweller, who himself had no access to land and could not produce his own food, to remain within the city. Tiny agricultural surpluses directly resulted in tiny urban populations. Nearly all Roman Britain's people were farmers.

Reece points out that in the eighteenth century William Marshall had noted that Cotswold farms varied in size between two hundred and one thousand acres; that five hundred acres might be considered a middle sized farm. Before going further, it is worth asking why the eighteenth century provides a good analogy for Roman Britain. Conditions were not precisely the same, but both societies were of the type termed 'pre-industrial'. Predating the industrial revolution, neither was subject to the massive changes in farming practice and rural occupation which the nineteenth century brought about. The eighteenth-century farmer had little more in terms of machinery or enhanced methods of production than his Romano-British counterpart; he was reliant largely upon his own labour and that of his draught animals, with access only to animal manure as a fertiliser. Broadly speaking, the same must have been true of Roman Britain. The Domesday Book (late eleventh century – a period again subject to the same sorts of constraints on farming practice as the second or eighteenth centuries) suggests that the lowest grade of family who might be expected to be self-supporting farmed fifty acres. One hundred acres, then, might support two families, and so on. Reece estimates land fit for farming in Britain at twenty million acres, and the average family at five people, giving a rough total population for the province of two million.[7] This whole process of estimation is founded upon later records and guesswork and there is plenty of room for error; but the process does provide a figure with which to conjure. One result of this calculation is that the presence of the Roman army added just two percent to the population of Britain. Each farmer, then, had only to work a little harder to provide enough agricultural surplus to feed the army. To see the real economic impact of the army we must look beyond the numbers.

Most obviously, soldiers of the Roman army were the destination for the vast majority of coins entering Britain. It was in coinage that their wages were paid; most of the civilian population would be lucky if they saw a handful of coins in their entire lives. For them most economic exchange was by barter. The few who handled coinage on a regular basis were shopkeepers in the towns and cities; merchants (who might sell to the army but also dealt with the city-dwellers and with the richer, landowning classes, who could afford to purchase the luxuries they had for sale) and finally those rich landowners themselves, many of whom would sell their agricultural produce to the army, either directly or through merchants. It is, therefore, in towns, at the rural villas of the rich and, of course, on military sites that archaeologists find most Roman coins.

This in itself means that the Roman army acted as an economic stimulus; it brought with it wealth in the form of large quantities of coin, making exchange far easier. Individual soldiers had considerable spending power; and their wealth was not in cattle, grain or land but in easily disposable cash. In areas where the army was stationed in numbers – as most obviously on Hadrian's Wall – there was a consequent concentration of cash. This attracted those with goods or services to sell, so that civilian settlements developed around forts. The Roman army also brought tax demands. The population of the empire in general was taxed for many purposes, chief among them to pay for the upkeep of Rome's huge standing army of professional soldiers.

Mention of tax moves us from the economy of Roman Britain and to her social structure. With the army came cities, which had an enormous impact on the way in which British society came to be organised. Stone-built cities were an alien transplant from the Mediterranean, from Greece and Italy, where city life was regarded as the most basic building block of civilisation. The etymological link between the Latin word *civitas* (city) and our *civilisation* is easy to see. Cities followed wherever the armies of Rome led, essential tools in the Romanisation of empire; they were the chief means by which native populations were integrated into Roman-style society. Most pragmatically, they were centres for administration and tax collection. More generally, on a social or cultural level, cities were centres from which Roman ideas of civilisation were disseminated to the local population. In terms of the social structure of the area around Hadrian's Wall, it is interesting that, while civilian settlements flourished around forts for much of the second and third centuries AD, only Corbridge developed into a town of any size and only Carlisle became a city. The social structure of the northern frontier differed from the social structure of the rest of Britain (see pp. 84-6 below).

The study of Hadrian's Wall

Just as Hadrian's Wall had a place in Roman Britain, so it also has a place in modern Britain. For at least four centuries it has been remarked upon, speculated about and recorded. The ruins we now see stretching between Carlisle and Newcastle, the books we read and the television programmes we watch about them, are the result of a centuries-long process of investigation. While remains of the wall, its forts and settlements, are now to a large extent static, preserved in their present state, our body of knowledge is not. It has advanced steadily over past centuries but there have been a number of key periods which have revolutionised study of the wall.

Our first records of Hadrian's Wall, as a curiosity rather than a functioning entity, come from the sixteenth century, which saw the emergence of the antiquary – the man of sufficient means to afford a life of scholarship, travelling the country (or even the world) recording ancient monuments together with local traditions about them. John Leland (? -1552) was the first of these to visit Hadrian's Wall and record his impressions, albeit briefly, in his *Itineraries*. He was followed by William Camden (1551-1623), whose *Britannia* gives a far fuller description of the wall. In 1695, a new edition of *Britannia* was published by Bishop Gibson; and that was followed in 1732 by the *Britannia Romana* of Revd John Horsley. This was extremely comprehensive, containing a largely military history of Roman Britain, together with an essay on the geography of the province and catalogues of inscriptions and sculptures. It says much for the visibility and reputation of Hadrian's Wall and the Antonine Wall at this time that Horsley's book also included chapters specifically dedicated to each of these two monuments and their forts; clearly, they were easy to study and held such a place in the public mindset that to ignore them would have been unthinkable in a work concerned, not specifically with northern Britain, but with the whole country. Shortly afterwards, in the 1750s, the wall-fort of Benwell and its bath house were planned and recorded by Robert Shafto.

Until the nineteenth century, then, it is clear that Hadrian's Wall was recognised throughout Britain as holding great significance for those interested in the country's Roman history. The fact that from the sixteenth century it was recognised as an important monument may be one of the reasons why, even though so many of the older buildings in the region of the wall are clearly constructed from dressed stone taken from it, so much of it has survived. There was certainly a market for books on the subject but the study remained purely topographical; in other words, it was concerned purely with the wall's appearance above ground. Archaeological excavation was not yet common. Nor was there any sense that ancient monuments should be preserved as a vital part of Britain's history. Men like Shafto, Horsley and Gibson were interested in physical manifestations of the past but others were not. The history of the fort of Chesters is a salutary reminder that we are, on the one hand, lucky to be able to visit Hadrian's Wall now and see so impressive a monument; that, on the other, it continued to evolve as part of a changing landscape even after the Roman army and administration had withdrawn from Britain.[8]

In 1796 the estate of Chesters, including the site of the wall-fort, was purchased by Nathaniel Clayton. As a typical eighteenth-century gentleman he created a parkland setting for his house; in so doing he had the 'eyesore' of what were apparently the extremely prominent and highly visible remains of the Roman fort levelled and grassed over. The grand setting for his house took precedence over his interest in the Roman past. That he had such an interest is clear, however, from his collection of Roman stones and antiquities, which he passed to his son John. Nathaniel died in 1832, leaving his collection and his house to John, who also inherited his father's antiquarian interests. In 1840 John Clayton began to excavate the fort of Chesters and for much of the ensuing fifty years devoted time and resources to studying and excavating Hadrian's Wall. Almost all of what we see at Chesters today is the result of his work (fig 3).

Fig. 3 The Commandant's House at Chesters fort

He also excavated the Housesteads and Cawfields milecastles and parts of the Housesteads fort. On his death in 1890, John Clayton owned five of the seventeen wall-forts and had taken steps to preserve them in the state in which they can be seen today. He also left behind him the large collection of sculptures and other finds, still displayed at Chesters, which his father had begun. Sadly he published very little of his research; almost all that we know is reconstructed from editions of Collingwood Bruce's *Handbook to the Roman Wall*. That this existed and was in use for so long is yet more evidence of the interest which Hadrian's Wall continued to excite in the general public during the later nineteenth and into the twentieth century.

The nineteenth century was, of course, the period in which excavation of the wall really began; interest had moved from recording its presence and its dimensions to studying it in detail. The intellectual descendants of Leland, Camden and the anti-quaries of the earlier nineteenth century discovered that digging holes could produce a wealth of information. This revolutionised study of the wall. One of its most obvious results was that not until the nineteenth century did it become generally accepted that it should be ascribed to Hadrian, rather than the third century emperor Septimius Severus. In the 1830s, Revd Anthony Headley produced new work where Horsley had left off, giving credit for the construction to Hadrian. He was an avid excavator, involved with digging both at Housesteads (where he worked on the temple of Mithras among other sites) and at Vindolanda.

Excavation of Hadrian's Wall continued throughout the nine-teenth century. The first large-scale excavation was in 1875, when fields in which the fort of South Shields lay began to be developed for housing. From this point, the pace of archaeological exploration accelerated; and by the 1930s chronologies for the development of most forts on the wall were clear. More recently, strict controls on excavation and general lack of funding for anything but rescue archaeology have meant that few excavations are being carried out. The privately-owned site and privately-funded work at Vindolanda is the single recent exception.

It is there that one of the more exceptional discoveries of the last half-century has been made – a discovery which has significantly advanced our knowledge of the northern frontier. As will become clear in the rest of this book, archaeology can answer many questions about Hadrian's Wall. In many areas of ancient study literary evidence provides complementary information when the two are used in proper conjunction.[9] Reliable literary evidence for any aspect of the wall other than the army is, unfortunately, lacking. The discovery made at Vindolanda, however, goes some way towards redressing this, even providing a level of information about daily life both on the wall and, more generally, throughout the empire, of the sort which few literary texts can supply. For example, the voice of a woman (rather than a woman's voice as reported by a male author) is scarcely ever found in texts surviving from the Roman empire to this day; yet among the Vindolanda tablets are several letters written by women.

The first tablets were found at Vindolanda in 1973. By 1994

two hundred and fifty had been unearthed; they make up three large published volumes, edited by David Thomas and Alan Bowman. Wood does not normally survive long in the ground and these tablets were made of birch, alder and oak; their preservation is due to the wet conditions at Vindolanda. Readers who have visited the site at times when excavation was in progress will recall looking into the archaeologists' trenches and seeing inches of standing water. A pain for the excavators, these conditions nonetheless preserve normally short-lived materials such as wood and leather (notably shoes) extremely well. The wooden writing tablets themselves are not entirely typical of the writing materials surviving elsewhere in the empire. From the deserts of Egypt come huge numbers of papyri; for hot, dry conditions preserve papyrus (a type of reed used as an early form of paper). Other areas with the same kind of wet conditions as Vindolanda have supplied writing tablets, usually two pieces of squared, hollowed wood, linked by a hinge. The hollowed interiors were filled with wax and a *stylus* (or pointed metal writing tool) used to scratch words into it. The wax could later be smoothed clear for re-use. The wax itself no longer survives but sometimes the stylus dug deep enough to leave its impressions on the wood, allowing us to read a few words. A number of tablets of this type come from excavations at Carlisle. The Vindolanda writing-tablets were in some ways similar but they did not provide a hollowed area for wax; they were written on directly in ink.

They reveal a curious mixture of written materials. They come from just outside a building which was firstly (*ca* AD 92-103) the commanding officer's residence, later a barrack block (*ca* 104-120) and finally workshops (*ca* 120-130). Some are personal letters, others either copies of official documents or notes that would later have been incorporated into permanent records. The most extensive group are associated with a man called Flavius Cerialis, who was prefect of the Ninth auxiliary Cohort of Batavians (see pp. 41-3 below for a discussion of military organisation) in the first years of the second century AD – commanding officer of the fort. Other groups are associated with Cerialis' wife, Sulpicia Lepidina, and with other officers. (Cerialis and Sulpicia are now central characters in Barbara Bell's *Minimus*, a Latin course for primary-age children who wish to start on the language and learn about the Romans, based on a cartoon mouse and set at Vindolanda in the officer's house.) It is clear that these documents were thrown away at some point (or points) – quite why is uncertain. Their value, however, is enormous and their discovery and study has revolutionised our understanding of Hadrian's Wall to almost the same extent as the first excavations of the nineteenth century. Thus, at the beginning of the twenty-first century, we have access to a wealth of new information which allows us to study the wall in much greater detail.

Chapter 2

Why build a wall?

Expansion of the Roman empire meant that its frontiers were continually moving outward. Before the end of the first century AD, they were rarely marked clearly on the ground, existing only as lines on maps. Hadrian, therefore, changed the Roman concept of a frontier to some extent when he constructed his impressive wall of stone between the Tyne and Solway rivers.

The concept of a frontier

The Romans believed that it was their destiny to conquer the entire world; they did not feel that their empire should be set within boundaries. The area under Roman control should keep expanding. This ideology is put into the mouth of Jupiter, king of the gods, by Virgil, effectively court poet to the emperor Augustus, in his epic poem *The Aeneid*. Jupiter is made to say that he has set no boundaries for the Romans; that they will conquer the world and create an empire which will last for ever.[10] The emperor was expected to ensure that this happened; Augustus, as the first emperor, was in effect defining the role. Virgil's comment, put into Jupiter's mouth, may be seen as a reminder to Augustus that, if he controlled the empire, then the Roman people expected him to expand it.

However, the empire had boundaries, even if they remained mobile for much of the first two centuries AD. While recognising that they might conquer the world and should not be restricted in doing so, Romans also realised that they lived within frontiers. Without them they could not have separated themselves from those whom their civilisation had yet to reach – the people whom Roman writers termed 'barbarians'.

The concept of the barbarian was one which the Romans

inherited from the Greeks. It appears again and again in Greek and Roman writing, becoming a literary trope, a device too often taken as fact. The Romans – and so too the Greeks – often defined themselves in terms of what they were not; they knew that they were civilised because they were not barbarians. This barbarian, non-Roman, image was projected onto peoples outside the empire. From time to time they raided the empire but they were not generally a warlike, barbaric menace which threatened the stability of empire and had to be kept out. The image of non-Roman peoples was constructed simply so that Romans could be sure who they were themselves. Sadly, however, many historians and archaeologists have not realised this and persist in seeing frontiers as fortified lines, watched ceaselessly to prevent barbarian hordes from breaking through and destroying the empire.

This misunderstanding of Hadrian's Wall is apparently supported by the *Historia Augusta*, the fourth century collection of biographies of various emperors (including Hadrian), which states that the wall was built to separate Romans from barbarians. Those who use this to support their argument that Hadrian built his wall to protect the empire fail to understand that the author of the *Historia Augusta* was not recording fact; rather he was simply stating the Roman ideological position – that Romans were different from barbarians, that the difference came about by virtue of the fact that the former lived within a civilised empire. Its boundaries, including Hadrian's Wall, separated them from their barbarian antitheses.

As Whittaker has pointed out, Roman frontiers did not really work like that at all.[11] They were not watertight dividing lines which no Roman or non-Roman tribesman could ever cross. Whittaker's work has, in recent years, led to a reassessment of the operation and function of Rome's frontiers. He has argued repeatedly that previous modern understandings of those frontiers were based on the model of frontiers to colonial states ruled by European nations in the eighteenth and nineteenth centuries. C.M. Wells, in an article effectively reviewing Whittaker's work, has supported its conclusions.[12] Wells, who wrote his doctoral thesis on Roman expansion before historians began to reassess ideas about the operation of the frontiers, interestingly says explicitly that as a postgraduate he had himself never thought to challenge received wisdom in the way Whittaker has done.

Before the 1970s, then, historians tended to see Roman frontiers as identical with the advanced military posts of modern empire: soldiers patrolled the frontier; they might raid the lands beyond in punitive actions. That was how the frontiers of British India worked in the nineteenth century and it was in those terms that nineteenth- and early twentieth-century historians understood frontiers. They were in the British empire linear barriers, intended to divide civilisation from barbarism, to hold back the forces of the latter; and thus the Roman world was understood in the same terms. Beyond the frontiers any Roman involvement was, therefore, seen as purely military, either small-scale raids to keep the barbarians quiet or large-scale invasions to push forward the frontier. In a few cases lands beyond frontiers might be 'client' kingdoms, whose rulers – like Herod of Judaea – maintained independence but paid homage to Rome. Hadrian's Wall was long regarded as a purely military frontier – not just soldiers but an entire wall supported by forts to keep the 'barbarian' non-Romans at bay.

So arose, too, the notion of a 'scientific frontier'. Whatever the Roman ideology of a conquered world, her expansion had to stop somewhere, if only briefly; so the Roman empire had frontiers. Those historians who saw them as impenetrable military barriers, naturally argued that Rome's frontiers should run along easily fortified lines, taking advantage of geographical features such as rivers and mountain ranges. So the Rhine and Danube frontiers were 'scientific frontiers'. The hills of the Tyne-Solway isthmus were regarded in the same way.

This militaristic line of argument is, however, based on a mis-understanding. Whittaker suggests that an analogy, far more useful than the British colonial model, is provided by the opening up of the American West.[13] The gradual westward thrust of the United States more accurately reflects Roman principles of expansion, by which frontiers are thus not fixed barriers but zones which encompass the current official line. Such a model is, indeed, the only reasonable way to explain the recent discovery of several fully Romanised towns, complete with typically Roman public buildings, north-east of the Rhine frontier in Germany. People were, it seems, arranging their lives around much the same social structures, whether they lived within the empire or just beyond its borders. On this model, Hadrian's Wall sat within a cohesive frontier zone; the areas immediately to the north and south of it had in common with each other far more than the area just south of the wall – one firmly Roman according to older models – had in common with Roman York or the Roman Cotswolds. It is worth exploring this line of thinking in a little more detail, although its emphasis on upon the practical working of the frontier ignores the wall's symbolic value.

The frontier zone was one of cultural and economic exchange.[14] To north and south of it, for example, people lived in similar types of house, used the same sorts of pottery, grew crops to supply the army. An official line between the Tyne and Solway rivers did not suddenly civilise those living to the south of it or make barbarians of those to the north. Roman jewellery and fine pottery associated with Roman-style dining have been found at a number of Scottish lowland sites – substantial stone roundhouses (as at Fairy Knowe and Leckie in Stirlingshire) or hill-forts (like Traprain Law in East Lothian). These appear to be the homes of a tribal elite; Roman goods were probably used there to demonstrate wealth and status, just as they were to the south in the villas of the Romano-British elite.

The number of crossing points on Hadrian's Wall meant that contact between north and south was straightforward; there is no evidence that soldiers stationed on the wall made any attempt to prevent local people from crossing to and fro. The use of Roman goods north of the wall suggests either that lowlanders crossed the wall to visit the markets in civilian settlements to the south, or that merchants travelled north. Evidence from Gaul suggests similar and regular movement across the Rhine frontier. One German tribe, the *Tencteri*, had access to Cologne provided they paid a fee; tribesmen crossing the frontier were generating income for the province. The *Hermunduri*, from beyond the Danube, also had trading rights within the borders of empire;[15] frontier zones, as Wells says, were zones for exchange.

The idea of a 'scientific frontier', chosen purely for tactical reasons, must be abandoned. As the presence of Roman goods and the existence of client kingdoms beyond them demonstrate, frontiers were created in the knowledge that Roman power and influence extended far beyond the boundaries of empire; they were constructed to permit the movement of people. This is not to say that decisions over their positioning were taken lightly; indeed Whittaker argues that the lines were chosen deliberately. It was not a case of Roman expansion simply running out of steam. Given the presence of the army – and the army had to be stationed on the frontier to allow onward expansion at a later stage (as the Roman ideology of a completely conquered world dictated) – it was economic factors that determined the positioning of frontiers. Put simply, the army had to be supplied. In the case of northern Britain, the Tyne-Solway line was ideal: the existing Stanegate allowed swift movement of goods along its length; the mouths of Tyne and Solway allowed access by sea for ships bearing goods and essential supplies; regions immediately north and south of the wall were agriculturally productive.

In practical terms, therefore, Hadrian's Wall was not a final frontier; it did not separate Romans from barbarians. The army was present on the wall; but it was there, arguably, to patrol and to control the region beyond rather than to hold the line in case of attack from the north of Scotland. The army of the wall (see pp. 41-4 below) was made up of auxiliary troops rather than the elite legionaries whom we might expect to find in a seriously threatened region. Yet we should not underplay the symbolic significance which the wall held in the Roman mind. For the Roman who lived, say, in Italy and never travelled to see the frontier in operation, Hadrian's Wall had a different value. Boundaries of every kind, from house walls to city walls, had enormous ideological significance; and the same was certainly true of the empire's frontiers in general – and the wall in particular. While Whittaker and Wells are right to argue that Roman frontiers did not mark the end of civilisation, that people on either side of the frontier did not differ in lifestyle, we may miss the symbolic importance of Hadrian's Wall, if we simply accept their line of analysis.

To stand on the wall even now is to feel a sense of endings. Even while we know that the ancient farmer to the south of the wall probably supplied the same markets as his neighbour to the north, was paid in the same coin, used the same farming techniques, ate off the same type of plates, and may even have been related to him, there is still a sense that stepping over the wall was a significant act. It was, theoretically at least, the end-point of Roman civilisation. It can be a struggle to reconcile this feeling with Whittaker's arguments. The Roman was, however, used to getting his mind round such contradictions. The city, for instance, was his centre of civilisation. Its wall enclosed and limited civilisation; everything beyond that was barbarism. Roman literature reinforces this notion repeatedly.[16] At the same time, however, the city extended beyond its walls; cities were surrounded by suburbs, in which people lived and worked. Indeed, in an attempt to reconcile the idea that the city walls encompassed the entire city with the fact that there were extensive areas of occupation beyond them, the city of Rome itself was forced during the third century AD to build a second set of walls (the Aurelian Walls) encircling a greater area. This is an isolated example but it exemplifies the attempt to reconcile practical and symbolic values; in most cases city boundaries simply had two different significances attached to them. Attitudes towards Hadrian's Wall may be seen in the light of those towards city walls. On the one hand walls and boundaries had real symbolic value; on the other, they functioned practically in a quite different way. What the Romans did was not always compatible with what they thought and wrote down: a boundary could have both a symbolic value *and* a practical mode of operating. Thus, Hadrian's Wall was practically a single point within a broad frontier zone *and* symbolically the end-point of civilisation.

The *vallum*

It is at this point that the *vallum*, the system of ditch and banks to the rear of the wall, should be discussed in more detail. It played a key role within the frontier system, in fact forming a frontier of its own. Much ink has been spilt on discussion and debate over its function. The fact is we cannot be absolutely certain what it was for.

The *vallum* is another case where the military bias of Romano-British archaeology, especially in the north of England (see also pp. 114-16 below), has distorted the evidence. Our discussion above has shown the error of seeing the wall as a military frontier

– soldiers defending it to stop barbarians getting in – rather than as part of a broad frontier zone. Yet a military role has also been suggested for the *vallum*, the ditch acting either as a last line of defence against attackers who had crossed the wall or as a means of keeping disaffected Romano-Britons away from the south side of the wall.

The first of these two suggestions may be completely dismissed. The wall was not itself a defensive boundary: there is real doubt that it had a fighting platform on top; in any case the Roman army was trained to meet its enemies not behind walls but on open ground. If the wall was not designed to be defended, the concept of the *vallum* as a second line of defence makes no sense at all. There is no access to the *vallum*: soldiers couldn't have got into it to defend it; the only defensible point would have been its southern bank, which would have meant yielding its northern bank to attackers. To build effective cover for an attacking force makes military nonsense. The alternative suggestion, however, merits more careful consideration.[17] The *vallum* was not easy to cross, save by its occasional causeways; at the very least it thus controlled movement of people to the wall itself and to the area north of it. If there *were* disaffected Britons south of the wall, then the *vallum* would have made it more difficult for them to attack the forts and milecastles of the wall. Still, I find it hard to believe that this was the reasoning behind the digging of the *vallum*; its southern bank would grant cover to attackers from the south every bit as much as the northern bank would protect a force who had crossed the wall from the north. If its function was to defend the rear of the wall, a ditch alone would have been the more sensible solution; the presence of the banks makes any defensive interpretation, whether from north or south, extremely unlikely.

The *vallum* does, however, fit a key part of Roman military ideology. As Breeze and Dobson point out, it creates an area south of the wall controlled by the army – a military zone. The ideology was keen to separate civilian from soldier: civilians, for instance, were not permitted to carry swords. The *vallum* may be seen as working in the same way; it separates a civilian from a military zone.

A more subtle example of the separation of soldier and civilian is the fact that in the Roman world armies could not normally enter cities. Here the symbolism of separation is crucial. The city wall defined a civilised area; beyond it was barbarism. On a grander scale, armies were forbidden to cross the Rubicon river into Italy; the Italian provinces were defined as purely civilian, except at clearly defined times (such as Triumphs). Thus, if an army could not enter the city or even Italy, more was going on in Roman thinking than a simple separation of civilian and military life. The army was removed from civilised life; its sphere of operation was effectively defined as the uncivilised. We must recall that this mentality developed early on in Rome's history, when the city was just a single city-state controlling only the area immediately around it (usually known as the hinterland). The development of an empire with frontiers, meant that the city-state ideology had become stretched to suit a larger compass. In many ways, as Rome grew in influence, the empire came to play the same role for Rome as the hinterland played for a small city.

We may also at this point consider the suggestion of Sir Ian Richmond that the *vallum* itself, rather than the wall, should be seen as the northern boundary of the province *Britannia* (or, later, *Britannia Inferior*).[18] There is no way of proving the truth of his suggestion but, if the *vallum* is seen as the dividing line between civilian and military zones, it certainly makes sense. The Romans had two definitions of land beyond city walls. Closest to the city was administered land under the city's control; beyond it and protecting it, was land which was not administered, known as *arcifinius*. Its role was to act as a sort of buffer, to protect (Latin *arcere* – the etymological link to *arcifinius* is clear) the administered land.[19] On a provincial scale, therefore, the city controlling the province and thus making the province into its administered land was London; then, once Britain was subdivided, York had responsibility for northern Britain. The ideology of controlled and uncontrolled land, then, applies to the relationship which these cities had with their provinces. If the *vallum* was the northern boundary of the civilian province, then the militarised zone beyond can be seen as *arcifinius*. This makes good sense: the army controlled the uncivilised area which was not under the direct administrative control of the city; and that area thus acted as a protective buffer for the civilian province. The delineation of a provincial boundary could only become physically visible in this way when a frontier was so carefully marked. So it is only in the case of Hadrian's Wall that we see the ideology of territorial domination so obviously evolving from that of the classical city-state to that of the Roman empire.

Hadrian

Hadrian's Wall represented a development – perhaps even a revolution – in designation and construction of a Roman frontier; it marked the border in very permanent terms. The reasons for its construction lie with Hadrian himself. Sadly, little can be known directly about his motives; our source material is simply too poor. Cassius Dio covered Hadrian in his history (written in the early third century AD) but the books which dealt with the emperor's reign survive only in fragmentary form. In any case, in common with almost every other historian of Rome, Dio was interested only in political details; the construction and operation of the wall were not a primary concern. At face value, the Hadrianic section of the anonymous fourth-century *Historia Augusta* should be of much more use. It gives a great deal more detail about Hadrian and the wall, even providing a motivation for its construction – to separate Romans from barbarians. The *Historia Augusta*, however, is hardy reliable. It was written for reasons relevant to fourth-century politics, dedicated to both the emperors Diocletian and Constantine. It may have been edited at least once before dedication to their memories. Whatever the precise truth, it seems to have been written for an imperial audience; and it has to be regarded as an instance of writing *exempla* – part of the tradition of using 'ideal types' of good and bad emperors, masquerading as fact, to educate the emperors of the writers' own day. Besides, it is known that the writer(s) were happy to fabricate official letters and documents, even make up events; on this basis, the *Historia Augusta* can be more or less dismissed as a source for Hadrian's Wall. It is telling that, so poor is the quality of our written evidence, until the nineteenth century, when archaeological excavation began to allow accurate dating, Hadrian's Wall was usually ascribed to the third century emperor Septimius Severus, who was known to have campaigned in Britain.

While our sources may not allow many conclusions to be

drawn about the wall itself, they do provide information about Hadrian's political position in Rome and about his rule of the empire. From this we can begin to work out why he might have built the wall. His decision was not taken in isolation; it should fit into the context of his other actions, about many of which we know far more, thanks to Cassius Dio.

Hadrian came to power in AD 117 on the death of the expansionist emperor Trajan. He had an immediate legacy of military success and glory to live up to. In addition, his very first act was to abandon Trajan's eastern conquests, seeing them as too difficult to hold – an act that cannot have been popular with powerful Romans who expected their emperors to expand – and certainly not shrink – the empire. What is more, Trajan had enjoyed good relations with the Roman senate and in many ways embodied the ideal Roman emperor – a modest way of life, devotion to his family, grand public works and, of course, his desire to expand the empire. Hadrian, on the other hand, spent much of his time in Athens rather than Rome. His love of all things Greek is shown in his building works there, in the statues which show him as a bearded Greek philosopher rather than a clean-shaven Roman general, and in his young male lover Antinous. The East, including Greece, had traditionally been viewed by the Romans as decadent and immoral, despite its culture; Greek values were regarded by many as the antithesis, in many respects, of those of Rome. Hadrian not only ostentatiously played the Greek; he did so by active rejection of key Roman values. Thus, in almost every way, he suffered by comparison with Trajan in the eyes of the powerful senatorial class.

His unpopularity is reflected in a conspiracy hatched by four ex-consuls at Rome, and in rumours that he was not in fact Trajan's chosen successor. The conspirators were captured and put to death on the senate's orders; Hadrian's rule was thus not actually threatened by the conspiracy, though it gives evidence of his unpopularity with at least some of the senatorial class. The rumours perhaps suggest a more subtle attempt to discredit him and weaken his position: an emperor was expected to choose his successor and, if Hadrian had not been chosen by Trajan, then the legitimacy of his principate was called into question. It seems not unreasonable to suppose that the army generals, drawn in most cases from the senatorial elite and accustomed in any case to the vast amounts of booty which campaigns to expand the empire brought, were just as unhappy as the senators.

Hadrian and the Wall

Hadrian's decision to build a wall in Britain has to be seen in light of the instability of his position. It might be argued that the move was nothing revolutionary; Trajan and Domitian had begun to use fortified lines to mark boundaries. Domitian began a line of forts along the German frontier between the rivers Main and Neckar; Trajan put palisades along the line of the Solway Firth and probably completed Domitian's German line of forts. There is, however, a real difference between a line marked in places by watchtowers or a mere wooden fence and a solid, permanent stone wall. A fence may be moved; its impermanence states that the boundary exists only for now. A high stone wall, on the other hand, has the appearance of a final, fixed boundary – one which, cutting a country in two, makes a far greater impression than a few miles of fence. Without the earlier attempts to mark a boundary with an actual physical line, the possibility of deliniating the frontier with a wall might not have occurred to Hadrian; but he took the concept much further, using it to make a lasting statement about the empire – and about himself.

In part, the weakness of Hadrian's position as emperor drove him to build the wall. Expansion of empire was part of the emperor's expected role. Hadrian was not in a position to expand, though he was still governed by the ideology that said he should. He was also following Trajan, who *had* expanded the empire. His position was comparatively weak. An alternative to becoming another emperor who expanded empire was to be the one who set its limits, who defined its final boundaries. The wall continues to set Hadrian apart nineteen centuries later. (Microsoft's spell-check recognises his name but marks Trajan as a mis-spelling!) If he could not expand the empire, he could definitively bound it and make a very physical mark upon it and upon history.

With the construction of the wall Hadrian also made a far more subtle statement, using stone almost as a biographical tool. In the ideology of empire, Augustus, the first emperor, was held to be the ideal. Published *ca* AD 121, the *Lives* of Julius Caesar and the first eleven emperors by Suetonius (*The Twelve Caesars*, tr. by Robert Graves [Penguin]) provide the classic example of this idealisation of Augustus. The twelve *Lives*, from Caesar to Domitian, were written by Suetonius, who himself held important posts in the imperial administation under both Trajan and Hadrian, to instruct subsequent emperors how to behave; foremost in their target audience must have been Hadrian. Augustus is presented as the standard, his ten successors as falling short of that ideal in some way, thus providing counter-examples. Crucially, it was Augustus who had said on his deathbed that the empire should not be further expanded but remain within its present frontiers. Perhaps stung by the publication of Suetonius' *Lives* – and certainly motivated by his politically weak position – Hadrian built the wall, marking one of the furthest frontiers of the empire. He made a statement in stone that he was living up to Augustus' injunction, marking himself out as the direct and rightful descendant of the ideal emperor.

But why in Britain? The island had, of course, provided easy glory for both Caesar and Claudius but the attention of the Hellenised Hadrian was generally fixed far more on the Greek East than on distant and peripheral Britain. The eyes of much of the empire rarely looked in that direction; such a building project might go unnoticed. At first glance, Hadrian's decision to build the wall is odd. It is possible that a war in Britain early in his reign may have prompted his action.

A number of pieces of evidence add up to make a war in Britain at some point between AD 100 and 120 a strong possibility. A fragment of a tombstone found at Vindolanda in 1997 mentions a war, though we cannot be sure of its date or whether it even took place in Britain: the officer commemorated in the inscription, a man called Titus Annius, though even the name has to be partially guesswork, may have fought the war elsewhere before being posted to Vindolanda, where his tombstone mentions his achievements. On its own the inscription tells us little; its information is too vague to support the weight of a definite conclusion. To it, however, can be added the tombstone of C. Julius Karus, who commanded the *cohors II Asturum* (a cohort of auxiliary soldiers drawn probably from north-western Spain); he was decorated in a British war and went on to become a senior officer in the legion *III Cyrenaica* in Egypt. We know that the *cohors II Asturum* were in Britain by AD 105 and that the *III Cyrenaica* had left Egypt by 128; so the inscription gives a time period of 23 years within which a British war could have taken place; the period was probably less, if we allow the officer time to have served in Egypt. The historian Cornelius Fronto, writing in the 160s, mentions a war in Britain under the emperor Hadrian, though he gives no sense of when during the reign it took place.

Fig. 4 A coin of Hadrian showing Britannia on the reverse

A coin of AD 119 (fig. 4) may place such a war early in the reign since it shows Britannia, the deity personifying the province of Britain; for Hadrian to associate himself with the province in this way would imply that he could lay claim to doing something significant in the province; on the basis of other coin issues for better documented wars and provinces, a military victory is the most likely explanation. A war, then, may well have been fought in Britain early in Hadrian's reign, presumably against rebelling tribesmen or against a large-scale invasion from the north.

For all this, a war hardly provides a cogent explanation for Hadrian's decision to construct the wall. It was a new development in the idea of a frontier; it very obviously separated empire from the barbarian regions beyond. For all that it was monumental and permanent, it could be crossed easily enough. It was not a defensive barrier; the Roman army was not designed to fight from behind walls but in open field (see p. 38 below). Thus, even if a war in Britain had resulted from Scots tribesmen raiding the empire, the wall would hardly be a valid response.

Besides we still cannot be absolutely certain that a war took place in northern Britain. Certainly the officer who died at Vindolanda may have been killed in a British war, in which case it is likely from his place of burial that it was fought in northern Britain; but the tombstone is too fragmentary for us to be sure that he was killed in the war mentioned; it could have been fought elsewhere earlier in his career, his death at Vindolanda being from some other cause. The Vindolanda tablets make no mention of a war: the only reference in them to British tribesmen is a sneering comment on their poor weaponry and tactics. While it might be argued that this implies battle, the context is only that of a memorandum – not a battle report, merely a statement that the local British (presumably north of the wall, where they were theoretically hostile) were no great threat. The assumption that Hadrian's Wall must be a defensive fortification tends to produce a false context: scholars, consciously or unconsciously, look for military action in association with the wall. In this case, the war could have been fought anywhere in the province; the tribesmen in much of northern Britain and in Wales especially were never fully pacified and Romanised. It could easily have been against them, as it had been only fifty years or so earlier under Agricola and his predecessors.

Hadrian visited Britain in AD 121-2; construction of the wall began after that and the timing can be no coincidence. Granted, Hadrian made tours of most of the provinces of empire but, if we accept the evidence for a war in Britain in the early years of his reign, then that would seem reason enough for his visit. If the war played a part in bringing him to Britain, then he could have seen for himself the opportunities which the Tyne-Solway frontier offered.

In practical terms Britain provided an ideal context for a statement of Hadrian's position. Being an island – and one not yet fully conquered – made it ideal. A short frontier of eighty Roman miles was easily fortified quickly and impressively. A similar project elsewhere could not have been so swiftly completed; nor could it have run along an entire frontier; its impact and its propaganda value would thus have been less. Though Britain was geographically peripheral, its very nature made it ideal for Hadrian's project.

The choice of Britain cannot, however, have been driven only by these practical considerations. The province's very marginality had an unexpected significance. While the courtiers who surrounded Hadrian in Rome and in Athens may never have thought about – much less visited – it, the island must have held significance for many senior soldiers. Under Hadrian one tenth of Rome's legions were stationed in Britain, together with considerable numbers of auxiliary troops. The army was generally an emperor's power-base; a man unpopular with the army could be quickly deposed, or at least have his position threatened. The army stationed in Britain in particular could have a disproportionate effect on politics throughout the empire. In AD 185, for instance, the British army mutinied; and in c. 196 (following the death of the emperor Commodus in 192) the British governor Albinus led troops across the Channel to face Septimius Severus, governor of Upper Pannonia (roughly speaking, modern Hungary), who claimed imperial status. Albinus was defeated but the episode reflects the potential power of the British governor and the army at his disposal. That power was more effectively asserted in the later third century; between 260 and 274 Britain formed part of the secessionist 'Gallic Empire'. The details are hazy; but it is enough in this context to say that the provinces and armies of Germany, Gaul, Spain and Britain withdrew themselves from rule by Rome for a short period, forming an empire of their own. Similar actions were repeated in the fourth century; a number of generals based in Britain – men such as Magnentius (AD 350-3) and Magnus Maximus (383-8) – aspired to become emperor and were supported by their troops. Most were ultimately unsuccessful but they still constituted a very real threat to the reigning emperors. Constantine the Great, the first Christian emperor, was in fact successful: proclaimed emperor by his troops at York in AD 306, he fought his way to Italy, then into the eastern half of empire, defeating all who opposed him. So, while Britain was indeed a small, distant province, the presence of so a large a proportion of the Roman army within its shores made it important to any emperor. In building the wall, Hadrian made a statement about his position as emperor to a group of potentially powerful and disruptive men. It is interesting to speculate about what might have been; speculation should never be taken as fact – many things *might* have happened in different circumstances – but it is tempting to wonder whether Hadrian, had he not taken such trouble to advertise his imperial credentials in Britain, might have faced mutiny and rebellion. The wall, therefore, emerges as a clever piece of propaganda, designed to show Hadrian as a worthy successor to the great Augustus and demonstrate his imperial credentials to the potentially troublesome army of Britain.

Chapter 3

Military life

From the end of the first century AD, when a clear frontier to the empire began to be formed between the Tyne and Solway, the Roman army had a significant impact on the region. It has been calculated, on the basis of the number of men each fort was intended to hold, that just over nine thousand men were stationed on the wall.[20] These men were not native to the area; they therefore boosted the size of the population considerably; they also had to be fed and supplied and, while supply networks for the troops on the wall stretched well into southern Britain, the first ports of call for soldiers with money in their pockets and for those supplying their official needs were local farmers and merchants. The impact this had upon the native population will be examined later (see ch. 4 below); here we concentrate on the army.

Legionaries and auxiliaries

The Roman army consisted essentially of two kinds of troops – legionaries and auxiliaries. We tend to associate legionaries, the quintessentially Roman soldiers, with Hadrian's Wall, though it was in fact auxiliary troops who were permanently stationed there, while the legions remained in their fortresses to the south. However, since it was men of the legions who actually built Hadrian's Wall – their involvement recorded by inscriptions found along its whole length – it is worth beginning with them.

Four legions were stationed in Britain during the initial occupation: at the end of the reign of the emperor Vespasian (AD 79) the *II Augusta* was stationed at Caerleon near Newport; the *II Adiutrix* at Chester; the *IX Hispana* at York; and the *XX Valeria Victrix* at Wroxeter in Shropshire. Reorganisation, probably under Trajan (the chronology is unclear, though his wars in the east would provide a good context for relocations) saw just three legions stationed in Britain. The *II Adiutrix* and the *IX Hispana* were both withdrawn from Britain; the *II Adiutrix* was certainly stationed on the Danube but the fate of the *IX* has attracted some controversy and is an issue worth brief examination. It used to be thought that the *IX* had marched into Scotland, perhaps with Agricola, and was lost. Rosemary Sutcliffe has provided an imaginary, fictional account of its end; and many claim to have seen the ghosts of its legionaries marching through the cellars of York. Certainly the legion disappeared from Roman records during the course of the second century; but inscriptional evidence suggests that it was simply transferred from Britain, continued to see action for some years and finally met its demise in Armenia during the 160s.

Under Hadrian the *II Augusta* remained at Caerleon; the *XX Valeria Victrix* had moved to Chester; the *VI Victrix* had arrived in Britain and was stationed at York. Detachments of all three were involved in building sections of the wall, though legionaries were rarely involved with it afterwards; only during times of trouble did they come north.[21] The exception to this is to be found at Corbridge, where men of the *VI* and the *XX* (during the second century) and of the *II Augusta* (during the third) were involved in industrial activities in the military compounds there.

The size of legions fluctuated throughout their history but by the reign of Domitian, just a few years before the building of the wall, numbers and organisation had settled into a regular pattern. The legion's strength was just over 5240 men, comprised of 5120 infantry and 120 cavalry – the latter used chiefly for duties such as scouting – plus their officers. As for internal organisation, the basic tactical unit was the century – originally 100 men but, by the first century AD, reduced to 80. For administrative purposes the centuries were arranged into 10 cohorts, each comprising six centuries, with the exception of the first, senior cohort, which had five double centuries, each of 160 men. Each century was commanded by a centurion. In total, there were 15,720 legionaries based in Britain under Hadrian, one tenth of the legionaries available to him empire-wide.

Although the legions began their existence in the early Roman republic as groups of amateur soldiers, farmers who fought for Rome in return for citizen rights, by the first century AD they were

Fig. 5 A Roman Legionary

completely professional. They were paid to be soldiers; and the population of the empire was taxed to pay and supply them. The legionary had time to be well-trained both in battlefield tactics and in more constructive activities. He was well-armed, with javelin and short-sword (fig. 5). The javelin (*pilum*) was for throwing. The sword (*gladius*) was simply for thrusting and was a key part of Roman military tactics. Celtic tribesmen whom the Roman army faced in Britain were often armed with swords up to three feet in length, which were used for slashing. This meant that each tribesman had to fight at least three feet from his nearest colleague to avoid risk of injury from their own weapons. The manoeuvres of legionaries, by contrast, were based on unity: as they fought side by side in close proximity, their great rectangular shields formed a wall; the infantry phalanx moved as one. The use of stabbing swords wielded from behind the shields meant the line was never broken in the way that the Celtic battle-line could be; also that the only people injured were the enemy. Roman shields were of wood, covered with leather; they had a metal boss to guard the hand; and they were light enough to be carried in one hand, though that meant they were only really proof against a slashing, glancing blow. Behind them, however, the legionary himself was well-armoured in a metal cuirass, helmet and reinforced leather kilt. Thus armed and protected, fighting as an ordered group, the legionaries could defeat far greater numbers of Celtic tribesmen.

Tactically the legionary was at his best in the open field; if the legions had to deal with a threat from beyond Hadrian's Wall, they would aim to do so either in front of it or some way behind it. The legionaries were also siege specialists, trained to attack an enemy behind a wall; they carried with them siege weapons such as catapults and battering rams. Significantly, they also provided the engineers of the empire. Trajan's Column, the unique sculpted monument in Rome which records the emperor's Dacian campaigns, for instance, has several illustrations of legionaries at work on bridges. It was for this reason that the wall was built by them and not by native labour. At face value this may seem a waste of trained men in the performance of back-breaking, menial toil; but it has to be remembered that such projects were an important part of the legions' role within a province. They were the very best labour available, their training ensuring that the wall-building project was completed by AD 138 at the latest and that its construction could be trusted absolutely.

The job of patrolling and guarding the frontier was left to auxiliary troops, suggesting that such duty may have been regarded as beneath the better trained legionaries. Originally, during the last two centuries BC, auxiliaries were recruited for two reasons – to increase the number of soldiers available to Rome and to provide various kinds of specialist troops. As the empire expanded, so did the number and range of troops available first to the senate, then (after Augustus) to the emperors. Auxiliaries were always recruited from outside Italy, from newly conquered territories. They were not citizens (until AD 212 when the emperor Caracalla extended citizenship to all free occupants of the empire); so their social standing was for most of the imperial period far lower. They were regarded as more expendable than legionaries and far less attention was paid to their training. At first they were used as specialist troops to augment the legions: cavalrymen from Gaul, Spain and the lands of the Danube frontier; slingers from the Balearic islands; archers from Crete and the Middle East. However, by the time Trajan's Column was erected, the role of the auxiliaries had progressed. Auxiliary infantry is shown on that monument taking prisoners, burning villages and fighting most battles; the legionaries are only shown constructing bridges, roads and forts or fighting the big, set-piece battles.[22]

So by the early first century AD auxiliaries were beginning to replace legionaries as the first soldiers to engage the enemy. From their origins – as largely untrained native troops, who fought using their own tactics and equipment – auxiliaries had progressed to the point where, trained more fully in Roman warfare and equipped in a similar way to the legionaries, they could be trusted to fight and win battles (fig. 6). Their presence on Hadrian's Wall meant they would almost always be the first force to engage an enemy coming from the north; for the nearest legionaries were at York, at least four days' march away. Ideally, the auxiliaries would stop the enemy, so that that none of the highly trained legionaries had to be risked; if they failed, they would at least thin out enemy numbers in preparation for the legions hurrying from the south; and, if killed, they were not as great a loss as legionaries. The presence of auxiliaries on the wall, however, also indicates that the role

Fig. 6 A Roman Auxiliary

of the army in the region was largely one of control. Auxiliaries patrolled the frontier zone, keeping the peace and reminding the local population of Rome's presence. Skirmishing – fighting small bands of raiders or malcontents – may have been a regular event; a strength report from Vindolanda records six men from the cohort stationed there as wounded, too small a number to be the result of a pitched battle, the possible result of a skirmish.

The organisation of auxiliary regiments was not as simple or standardised as that of the legions; their units varied in strength and composition. Trajan could call on thirty legions; he also had at his command something in the region of 440 auxiliary regiments, whose combined manpower outnumbered the legions by between a third and a half. Under him fifty to sixty auxiliary regiments were stationed in Britain.[23] These were constituted in a variety of different ways: the largest groups of infantry were called cohorts and, as in the legions, these were subdivided into centuries. The most common type of auxiliary cohort was the *cohors quingenaria peditata* – one divided into six centuries each of eighty infantrymen. Q*uingenaria* implies a cohort of five hundred men but six centuries of eighty gives a total of four hundred and eighty. The discrepancy is simply explained: the extra twenty men were officers and headquarters staff. While units of this type were common throughout the empire – one hundred and thirty have been counted in the mid-second century[24] – only three have been identified on Hadrian's Wall: at Housesteads, Great Chesters and Birdoswald.[25]

A larger version of these units, the *cohors peditata milliaria*, existed but was far less common. In the mid-second century only eighteen are known in the empire as a whole. In theory *milliaria* should mean that these cohorts had one thousand men. However, the strength report for the First Cohort of Tungrians, recorded on one of the tablets found at Vindolanda (fig. 7), gives a total of seven hundred and fifty two men, close to the eight hundred which would be produced by ten centuries of eighty men (ten 'centuries' explaining the designation *milliaria*). Certainly this cohort was too large to be anything other than a *cohors milliaria*. It was clearly below strength but by how much is uncertain: a shortfall of close to fifty men would seem more reasonable than one of two hundred and fifty.

Much more common on Hadrian's Wall than either of the

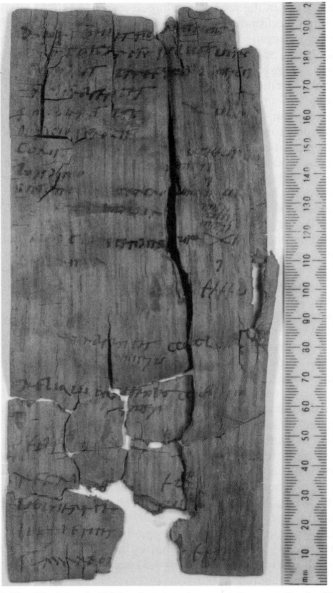

Fig. 7 The Vindolanda Tablet showing the strength report for the First Cohort of Tungrians

above types of infantry cohort was a mixed unit of infantry and cavalry, known as *cohors equitata*. Cohorts of this kind should not be thought of in the same terms as dragoon regiments in more modern armies, men trained to fight as *both* infantry and cavalry. Roman auxiliary units of this type were, rather, a genuine mixture of troops: infantry who fought as infantry, cavalry who fought as cavalry. They were thus extremely flexible and that fact alone explains their predominance on the wall. They comprised six centuries of infantry (four hundred and eighty men, if their centuries were the same as those of other auxiliary cohorts) and four troops (*turmae*) of cavalry (one hundred and twenty eight men), giving a total of six hundred and eight soldiers, plus officers and headquarters staff. A handful of examples, however, suggest at face value that this figure may be too high, that an estimate closer to the five hundred, suggested by the designation of these cohorts as *quingenaria*, would be more accurate. For instance the *cohors I Hispanorum veterana* (from Spain) had five hundred and forty six men, of which four hundred and seventeen were infantry; the *cohors I Augusta praetoria Lusitanorum* (from Portugal) had five hundred and five men, three hundred and sixty three of them infantry; and an unnamed cohort had four hundred and eighty seven men, three hundred and fifty of them infantry.[26] A better explanation, however, is that the disparities in these figures, like the under-strength Tungrians recorded at Vindolanda, suggests that all these units were simply below strength; the cohort of Spaniards has far too many men for any other explanation to be likely. Mixed cohorts were found at nearly every fort on Hadrian's Wall save the four already mentioned (Housesteads, Great Chesters, Birdoswald and Vindolanda) where unmixed infantry units were stationed.

There were also three other exceptions. The units at Chesters, Stanwix and Benwell were rare units composed purely of cavalry, known as *alae* (lit. 'wings'). The one at Stanwix was the largest cavalry unit in Britain. Most of these units had sixteen troops (*turmae*) of thirty two men, giving a unit strength of five hundred and twelve; that at Stanwix had twenty four troops, so that the *ala* there had in theory seven hundred and sixty eight men.

It is worth taking a little time to think about the deployment of troops on the wall. Cavalry, infantry and mixed units were not arranged randomly; a tactical scheme can be discerned. The three wall-forts in which infantry were stationed – Housesteads, Great Chesters and Birdoswald – are side by side close to the centre of the wall. It is not, however, this central position that is particularly significant; rather that this stretch of the wall is the highest and lies along an escarpment. While men could find paths down into the countryside north of the wall – plenty of these are used by modern walkers – horses could not. There was, therefore, no point in stationing any kind of cavalry in these forts. The fourth fort containing an infantry unit was Vindolanda; it lies immediately south of the above three wall-forts, so that the same reasoning applies.

Far better conditions for the operation of cavalry are to be found in the regions of Stanwix, Benwell and Chesters. North of Stanwix lies the Solway Firth – flat ground on which cavalry could be used to best effect. The same holds true for Benwell, close to the Northumbrian coast. Chesters, lying some way inland, is a somewhat different case; there is no coastal plain here. Instead it is on the North Tyne river in a broad valley which extends some way to the north – once again ideal country for cavalry. The conditions at Benwell and Stanwix apply to other forts, such as Carlisle on the west coast or Wallsend on the east.; they were home, not to cavalry, but to mixed units. The explanation is in part that *alae* were rare; to find three in such close proximity is in any case unusual. Moreover, in the event of invasion from the north, Roman military tactics would have relied largely on infantry to do most of the fighting. The *alae* would need infantry support and this would come first from other forts nearby.

Along the rest of the wall mixed units suit the conditions well. The role of cavalry in battle is considered below (pp. 46-7); their presence as part of a mixed unit gave the fort's garrison greater flexibility in policing the regions north of the wall. Able to travel further and more quickly than infantrymen, cavalry could ensure a regular Roman presence some way outside the boundary of Roman Britain. Meanwhile the presence of infantry ensured that more difficult terrain could also be patrolled.

In terms of the manning of the forts of Britain's northern frontier, the strength report of the Tungrian cohort at Vindolanda is interesting. Most obviously, the report makes it clear that the theoretical strength of a unit did not necessarily match reality. The

Tungrians were short of at least forty eight men, perhaps through death – natural or in minor skirmishes – or through retirements. The report is also important because of the numbers it gives for soldiers present and available for service. The total for absentees is four hundred and fifty six, including five centurions. Men were dispersed throughout Britain; three of the place-names on the tablet have been lost but one centurion was for some reason in London. Three hundred and thirty seven men, including two centurions, were at Coria (presumably Corbridge). Some of them may have been on leave – another Vindolanda tablet is a request for leave at Coria – but, however peaceful the times, it cannot be the case that well over half the cohort's strength was permitted to be on leave. Most of them must have been deliberately posted away; the natural assumption would be that Vindolanda must have been manned by men from other cohorts. Perhaps the intention was to keep men moving around to prevent boredom and allow them to become familiar with another area; should the Tungrians, for example, be either posted as a whole to Corbridge or called upon to fight in that area, men familiar with the locality would be an advantage.

Auxiliaries were generally paid less than legionaries. In AD 84 army pay was reassessed and it is those pay-scales which applied to the first troops stationed on the wall. A legionary was paid twelve *aurei* (gold pieces) a year, in instalments. An auxiliary foot-soldier, by contrast, drew ten *aurei*, while cavalrymen in the part-mounted cohorts drew twelve, on a par with the legionary. Best paid of all was the cavalryman in the *ala*; he earned fourteen *aurei* a year. This is slightly odd: the legionaries were of a higher status but earned no more than auxiliary cavalrymen. This might be explained by arguing that the pay differential was because cavalry were expected to pay the upkeep of their horses, though it is hard to believe that this was more expensive in the *alae* than in the mixed cohorts. The higher pay for cavalry must reflect the value placed on cavalry by the Roman army (see pp. 46-7 below).

From the soldiers' pay, deductions were made to cover a range of goods; according to a papyrus document of AD 81 found in the Egyptian desert, money was taken for hay, food, boots, socks, clothing and the camp Saturnalia.[27] It is a little difficult to assess ancient money in modern terms. The best that can be done is to point out the ancient cost of goods readily available in the modern world. For example, according to sums of money recorded in the Vindolanda tablets, a towel might cost two *denarii*, a tunic three. There were twenty five *denarii* to the *aureus*; each *denarius* was divided into sixteen *asses*.

Auxiliaries were, by the time of the wall, armed and trained in a way similar to legionaries (fig. 7). Infantry shields were not rectangular but oval and as such may have offered slightly less protection at top and bottom; auxiliary infantry also wore mail rather than the cuirass, again perhaps slightly less effective than legionary equipment. Cavalry were armed with long swords designed for slashing rather than stabbing; the short sword (*gladius*) would have given a cavalryman little reach and, in any case, cavalry combat was not reliant upon close-order manoeuvres in the way of infantry phalanxes. Rather than advancing upon the enemy behind a wall of shields, the cavalry would aim to outflank him, attacking the unprotected backs and sides of his formations.

There is debate as to how effective cavalry could be in battle; without stirrups (unknown in the ancient world) the cavalryman, to maintain his balance, was reliant on high pommels in the front and rear of his saddle. There must be some doubt whether balance could be maintained easily, whether cavalry could be as useful in the heat of battle as, for example, mediaeval knights may have been. However, the broad saddle gave plenty of support and the combined weight of man and horse could probably be controlled effectively. If so, then cavalry could do significant damage to an infantry unit. It was, arguably, not until the invention of the pike that infantry could effectively repel a charging cavalry unit; for against shorter weapons the sheer weight of a galloping horse will break any line of infantry. (For those keen to experiment with balance, there is in the Tullie House Museum in Carlisle a replica saddle which may be mounted.)

The higher rates of pay for cavalrymen may, therefore, reflect their greater value in battle; and their presence in large numbers on the wall itself reflects their usefulness in the terrain and the circumstances prevailing in the frontier zone. Their prominent presence could perhaps be explained away in terms of their value as scouts, though the numbers seem too great for that. The wall was, after all, not intended as a defensive barrier (see ch. 2 above)

but as a frontier with lands beyond which would be regularly
patrolled. The forces there were also the first line of defence for
Roman Britain; the cavalry must have been expected to fight
effectively.

Supplying the army

To supply the army on Hadrian's Wall was a considerable under-
taking. As already observed (see pp. 11-12 above), feeding Britain's
Roman army necessitated only a small increase in agricultural
production from each farmer but that additional output had to
be collected, then transported to the soldiers. The presence on
Hadrian's Wall of around 9000 men, together with units stationed in
the forts of the Stanegate – something in the region of 3000 to 3500
men, assuming that each of the forts contained a unit of 480 to 600
men, while Vindolanda contained a *cohors milliaria* – meant that a
lot of food had to be transported to the frontier. Rough estimates of
the amount of grain needed by a soldier to make bread, combined
with results from wheat grown using (so far as possible) ancient
farming techniques, suggest that a single *cohors quingenaria*
(nominally 480 men) would need seven hundred acres to supply
it with wheat for a year.[28] The figure would be higher for units
including cavalry, since the horses needed feed as well as the men.
Seven hundred acres, of course, could never be given over entirely
to a single unit: those who worked the land had to be fed first.
This sounds a huge amount but Britain could obviously supply the
army of the province quite easily; the historian of the later fourth
century, Ammianus Marcellinus, records that in his own century,
when invasions of the Rhineland had left the fields devastated,
British grain was transported to the garrisons of the Rhine.[29] Yet,
even if there was plenty of grain, it still had to be collected and
transported to the army in general and to the forts of Hadrian's Wall
in particular. And it should not be forgotten, that grain was only part
of the picture; the army of the wall also needed other foodstuffs,
clothes, armour, weapons, pottery, luxury goods and so on.

The mechanics of providing for the army worked in a variety
of ways. According to the historian Tacitus, much of the taxation
of the empire's population was in grain, not in cash.[30] Most, if not
all, of that grain went straight to the army. Goods could also be

requisitioned, provided the soldier or agent held a permit allowing them to carry out requisition. In this case a set price would be paid; it did not reflect market-price; so farmer or merchant might profit or might lose on his goods. Supplies could also be bought directly on the open market: depending on market-prices that might produce for farmer or merchant a deal that might be better or worse than having his goods requisitioned. It may also be that the army owned land of its own, albeit not necessarily close to the forts. An imperial lead seal, used to seal official government documents, found in fourth-century levels at Boxmoor villa in the Chilterns, suggests state ownership; the chief destination for state-produced goods was the army. Certainly state-owned factories in several of the cities of Gaul appear to have existed primarily, or even entirely, to supply the army; one at Trier, for example, produced shields, while a factory at Arles produced armour just for officers. There is so far no evidence for similar factories in Britain; either the Gallic factories supplied the British army or there were similar ones in Britain, as yet undiscovered.

Markets, merchants and farmers who supplied the army were both local and based further afield. Evidence from elsewhere in the empire suggests that military units might make use of agents or even develop contracts with individual suppliers. Residues of olive oil tend to cling to pottery, allowing identification, not only of amphorae used to transport oil, but also of different oils; finding amphorae which contained similar oil in two different places suggests a link between those places. Study of amphorae found at forts on the Rhine frontier and in Spain has shown that there were links between various forts and specific oil shippers or estates (depending on whether it was the estate or the shipper who put the oil into the amphorae) in Spain. In addition, a papyrus from a military unit in the province of Moesia on the lower Danube records the use of agents to secure supplies from Gaul. Throughout what was the Roman empire are found the tombstones of men termed negotiators (*negotiatores*), who were involved in trade; that they are found more often along military supply routes (in Arles or Marseilles, for instance, or in the cities of the Rhine frontier), suggests that they played a role in supplying the army.[31]

Moving from this general picture to the specifics of supplying the wall-forts, we again find our best evidence at Vindolanda. There

is, unfortunately, little from other forts; so we are left to assume that the picture presented by the Vindolanda tablets was typical. One tablet provides a list of people, sums of money and, in some cases, commodities. Its interpretation is not entirely clear but it appears that certain people provided goods, presumably for the fort, and were then paid. Felicio the centurion, for example, has next to his name records of forty five pounds of bacon, fifteen and a half pounds of bacon lard and various sundries, for which he received a total of fourteen *denarii* and four and three quarter *asses*. Perhaps it was part of his duties to acquire goods for the fort; so here we may see, in these few lines, the requisition system in action. Two lines above Felicio is Sabinus, recorded as being from Trier in northern Gaul. No specific commodities are recorded by his name, only the sum of money paid to him, thirty eight and a half *denarii* and two *asses*. It is a considerable sum – over a month and a half's pay for a legionary; so the goods involved were either too numerous to write down, or they were supplied on a regular basis and did not need re-recording. That Sabinus was from Trier may indicate that he was an agent for the fort and secured a supply of goods from northern Gaul. Equally, however, there is evidence that many foreign merchants lived in the civilian settlements around Hadrian's Wall (see pp. 67-70 below); so Sabinus may have been a local merchant, known in the area by the fact that he had come originally from Trier.

Certainly, a great deal of the food and many of the goods which the garrisons of the northern frontier needed were supplied locally. The Vindolanda fort, as the instance of the centurion Felicio shows, obviously had access to local sources of goods. Some of these were owned by the fort itself: one tablet records quantities of wheat sent to (among others) Lucco, who was in charge of the pigs, and to the oxherds. The fort would not have been providing wheat to local farmers without an explanatory comment in the records – as shown by the fact that the same tablet records wheat sent to a man named Felicius Victor as a loan. So the wheat sent to swineherds and oxherds demonstrates that the fort itself owned pigs and oxen. Oxen, of course, were not primarily for eating; they were draught animals, used to pull ploughs and the carts which were the main heavy transport. We cannot know whether these oxen were for ploughing but mention of them raises the possibility that the fort also owned fields which it cultivated.

At both Chesters and Great Chesters remains of water mills have been found; the one at Great Chesters may have been owned by anyone but the situation of the mill at Chesters suggests that it was owned by the fort. The leat supplying the mill's water runs through the base of the east tower and through the approach ramp to the road bridge; implying that mill and fort were built at the

Fig. 8 The military granary at Corbridge

same time as part of a unified plan and demonstrating that at some forts, at least, the garrison could grind its own flour. The origin of the grain is less clear. All forts had their own granaries to store grain until it was needed; one of the best preserved granaries is at Corbridge (fig. 8). One letter at Vindolanda is a plea for cash to pay for grain (and other goods) which had been ordered; it was, however, sent *to*, rather than *from*, Vindolanda, perhaps implying that Vindolanda was functioning as some sort of supply base for the further dispersal of goods to other places.

In this context the fort at South Shields provides interesting evidence; for it was developed in a unique way during the course of the third century. Built as an ordinary fort in the 160s, it was adapted as a supply-base (*ca* 205-7), doubtless because of its position at the mouth of the Tyne. From this date, it contained thirteen granaries,

giving a capacity for two thousand and eighty one tonnes of grain. Later (*ca* 222-35) seven more granaries were built, raising capacity to three thousand, three hundred and sixty three tonnes. Evidently, much of the grain for the frontier garrisons was transported to South Shields and stored there prior to distribution. Other facilities at Corbridge and perhaps at Maryport on the west coast may have performed similar functions or simply served as further storage points in a network emanating from South Shields.[32] At the very least, it is possible to say that the fields immediately north and south of the wall were not required to supply all the grain needed by the frontier forts.

Whether they owned their own fields or not, the forts on Hadrian's Wall certainly had their own workshops. Corbridge had entire enclosures dedicated to industrial production of military equipment during the third century, when the civilian settlement had also grown into a town. The presence of legionaries running these operations, together with their scale, suggests considerable specialisation. The workshops probably supplied far more than one fort. At Carlisle, too, the first-century fort has produced evidence of armourers' workshops. Again, the Vindolanda tablets provide more details. On the 25th of April, in an unnamed year, three hundred and forty-three men are listed as being in the workshops: twelve were shoemakers; eighteen are described as builders to the bath-house; and there are also mentions (in very vague terms) of lead, wagons, kilns, clay, plasterers, tents, rubble – and of a hospital. For all its vagueness, the list nonetheless gives an idea of industrial activities carried out by the Vindolanda garrison – and so, presumably, by other garrisons along the wall.

The civilian settlements surrounding the frontier forts contained many merchants (see pp. 67-70 below). It is clear that the wages paid to soldiers ensured that a cash rather than a barter economy could flourish in the area; it was this that supported a merchant class. To what extent they dealt directly with soldiers, to what extent with people who also relied on the army for an income (local farmers, inn-keepers, prostitutes and so on) cannot be gathered from the available evidence. There was certainly a market for luxuries, both locally produced and imported from abroad; trade in them was supported, in one way or another, by the cash paid to soldiers. There is plenty of evidence for local industry in the *vici* (civilian settlements) close to Roman forts. Iron, copper, silver and gold were all worked, to produce necessities like tools as well as luxuries such as jewellery. Lists of goods from Vindolanda sometimes include single items like tunics and towels, which may well have been bought locally. One lucky soldier was sent socks, underpants and sandals, apparently by his mother; since such items were evidently not supplied by the army, other soldiers may have had to buy them locally.

Goods also came from further afield. One of the Vindolanda tablets presents us with a shopping list sent to a slave; sadly, we do not know where the slave was based or where he was instructed to do his shopping. But, as the list is entirely of fresh produce, he cannot have been far from Vindolanda. He is asked for commodities in considerable quantities and it seems unlikely that this was a private commission – rather for the fort as a whole. Twenty chickens are requested, for example, together with a hundred apples and one or two hundred eggs. If Felicio provides evidence for the requisition system in action, then the slave's shopping list is more likely to represent purchase on the open market. The slave was acting in some way as an agent for the fort.

More definite mention of an agent is found in another tablet, though his location is again unclear. Metto has written to Advectus, presumably a soldier at Vindolanda, to say he has sent various wooden goods through the agency of Saco. The best interpretation is that Saco had responsibility for the transportation of the items, while Metto had either bought them or supplied them himself. The number of items is too great for a private contract; so the consignment must again be for the fort – thirty-eight cart axles, thirty-four wheel hubs and three hundred spokes, together with a number of other wooden objects and six goat-skins.

Amphorae (large pottery jars) found on the wall indicate long-distance supply. If Sabinus was an agent in Trier, then he may have been responsible for this sort of activity on behalf of Vindolanda. As already mentioned (p. 48 above), traces of the amphora-content can still be found on their remains, allowing us, as on the Rhine frontier, to build a picture of supply networks stretching across the empire. Wine, olives, prunes, olive oil, even cough mixture were transported to the British frontier from Italy, Spain and Gaul. Fish-sauce and salt came down the Rhine and across the North Sea; Roman inscriptions from what is now the Dutch province of Zealand give thanks to the local goddess Nehallenia for the safety of both ship and merchant, indicating that some made a livelihood out of shipping goods to Britain. They were not, in other words, locally produced but they were either, as in the case of salt, an absolute necessity or, as in the case of the fish-sauce, hugely popular with the army in particular. Thus the concentration of soldiers on Hadrian's Wall had an economic effect on other areas of the empire.

Some pottery, particularly the extremely fine red glazed ware known as 'Samian' or 'Arretine ware', was transported from Gaul and Italy. Other pottery used by the army came from within Britain but still travelled some distance to reach the wall. Kitchen and table wares were in greatest demand; they came from the south, where the best supplies of clay were situated. Pottery commonly found at the western end of the wall came all the way from south east Dorset in some quantity, while the eastern end was supplied on a large scale by kilns in Essex and north Kent. The fact that these types of pottery are rarely found on sites away from Hadrian's Wall (and the Antonine Wall) suggests that they were produced pretty much exclusively for the army of the north. This must be an example either of factories owned by the army, or of a direct relationship between the pottery producers and the forts of the wall, which resulted in particular kinds of pottery sold as a monopoly to the frontier garrison. The second is perhaps the more likely; if the army owned the factories, then we might expect the pottery types to be found more widely on other military sites in Britain. The demands of the army on the wall had an economic impact in all these ways on the frontier zone, on the rest of Britain, even on the rest of the empire.

Social life

Soldiers spent much of their time involved in military activities, which might include patrolling the frontier zone, training and perhaps, given the number of men listed in the workshops at Vindolanda, being involved in assorted industrial tasks. But they were given time off duty; and this allowed for the development of a life in and around the wall-forts which may be broadly described as 'social'. The growth of the *vicus* (civilian settlement), will be discussed later (pp. 65-73 below); we are concerned here with those activities in which the soldiers were directly involved.

What they did when not on duty is by no means always clear. The *vici* must have contained bars, inns and brothels – places where soldiers could relax and spend their wages; but there is no direct evidence of such activities in the area of the wall. They may be safely assumed but cannot be proven. Leave was a possibility, though it is likely that soldiers on leave did not travel very far. The application for leave at Corbridge found among the Vindolanda tablets demonstrates that they might merely visit the next fort or the one beyond; and that is hardly surprising, given the slowness of ancient transport. Newcastle to Carlisle, an easy drive by car, was a trip of several days on foot or by cart. Mention of Corbridge as a place to spend leave must beg the question whether some of the three hundred and thirty seven men of the Tungrian cohort listed as

Fig. 9 Part of the bath house at Chesters

posted there were actually on leave. Self-evidently most of them cannot have been, since they represent nearly half of the cohort's strength, but possibly a few were. Corbridge may have offered a welcome change of scene: there was a large *vicus*; perhaps the shops, bars and brothels there were better.

For the soldier simply off-duty, a number of activities were available. Close to each fort, apart from the assumed attractions of the *vicus*, there were the baths (figs 9 and 10). Communal bathing was an important part of Romanised life. It offered an opportunity to relax and to gossip with friends. Dice and gaming cubes found in the baths at Vindolanda suggest that playing games was an

Fig. 10 Niches for the original wooden lockers in the changing room at Chesters bath house

important part of this relaxation. It should be remembered, too, that Northumbria can be bitterly cold; the heated rooms of the bath house, kept warm by the hypocaust system (the circulation of hot air through hollow floors and walls) doubtless offered oases of warmth to off-duty soldiers.[33] Gaming counters and dice are regular finds also within the wall-forts; bored, illiterate soldiers obviously spent a great deal of their spare time on such distractions.

Hunting was also a regular activity; local game included boar, wolf, bear and deer. One of the Vindolanda tablets, clearly a copy of a letter written by Flavius Cerialis, commanding officer of the fort between *ca* AD 97 and 103, requests some hunting nets from his brother Brocchus. Small altars to a variety of gods are frequently found along the wall, each with a hollow in the top to receive libations of wine or oil poured in honour of the god. Many of them are associated with success in hunting; the god is being thanked for a good day's bag. A common god in this context is the local north British deity Cocidius, sometimes found associated with Mars; Cocidius was a god of both war and hunting.

Religion played a large part in the soldier's life. Many units brought their home deities with them to Britain: Mars Thincsus (a combination of the Roman Mars and the German deity Thincsus), for example, appears at Housesteads. At an official level prayers for the safety of the emperor, recognising his divinity, would be a regular occurrence. Yet it remains the small personal cults that cut most ice with the men. One of the most interesting examples of Roman military religion is the cult of Mithras, which was almost unique in not admitting everyone. We know little about Mithras, since his cult was a 'mystery religion'. As in the cults of Isis and Cybele, worshippers were forbidden to make any record of the religion or its practices, or even mention them to the uninitiated; so in the case of Mithras we have little more than the name, some excavated temples and some sculptures. Worship of Mithras came from the east, brought to Rome by merchants; it was adopted by the officer class of the Roman army. Its temples are always small, reflecting the limited membership, always partly underground as if false caves, and always just outside the fort (figs 11 and 12). Mithras seems to have been a sun-god or he was at least associated with the sun. Visitors to the Mithras temple at Carrawburgh will note the hollow altar, within which a candle was placed so that its light would shine out as a representation of the sun (fig. 13). Temples to Mithras (Mithraea) have been found at several of the forts on the wall, including Housesteads and Carrawburgh, the latter partially reconstructed. Only officers could be members of the cult, though there can have been nothing secret about its existence because the temples are not hidden; and there are numerous references to Mithraism in Roman literature.[34]

Membership of the cult no doubt gave Roman officers a social network on which they could draw. The Vindolanda tablets reveal

Fig. 11 The Mithraeum at Carrawburgh

Fig. 12 Detail of the three main altars from the Mithraeum at Carrawburgh

Fig. 13 The Altar of Mithras from Carrawburgh

another kind of social network. The letters of Cerialis and of his wife Sulpicia Lepidina provide a partial picture of the social life of a senior officer and his family. Brocchus, addressed as his brother, has already been mentioned; his letters to Cerialis appear occasionally. More frequent are those between their two wives. Where Brocchus was stationed is not known; it may have been somewhere with a better market, since Cerialis requested not only hunting nets. One tablet gives an inventory of household goods, including several types of tunic (e,g, half-belted, or tunics specifically for dining);

Fig. 14 A Roman woman of high rank

they came from Brocchus. A letter from Brocchus and a certain Niger wishes Cerialis well in some unidentified endeavour, promising that he will be meeting quite soon with the governor. This might almost be interpreted as patronage in action; the connection between the governor and Cerialis' endeavour might suggest that Niger and Brocchus were arranging for Cerialis to meet the governor. Governor of what, we do not know, though the obvious explanation would be the provincial governor, with the

Fig. 15 The Vindolanda Tablet showing Claudia Severa's birthday invitation

implication that Brocchus and Niger had influence at the top of the administrative hierarchy.

The letters between Sulpicia Lepidina and Brocchus' wife Claudia Severa are informative at a more private level. They reveal a personal relationship between two women, both of whom may well have been lonely. Cerialis commanded a fort; Brocchus, too, was evidently a military man of at least similar status; their wives would thus be somewhat isolated by their considerable social status (fig. 14). They will have had few women of similar status, with whom they could communicate closely. The letters between them deal with little things, such as invitations to come and visit: Claudia, for example, invites Sulpicia to visit her on her birthday (fig. 15). Another letter reveals that the women had

Fig. 16 The bear cameo, presumed to have originally come from a
brooch, found at South Shields

few freedoms: Claudia has to ask Brocchus' permission before
going to stay with Sulpicia. And the letters between the two are
also almost always counter-signed by their husbands, who briefly
add their greetings. On a mundane level this might represent
typical male disinclination to write letters of their own, except that
we *have* letters between them; so the counter-signing appears to
be a way for the husband to check on and approve the letter and
its content.

These women at least had the benefits of a legal marriage,
wealth and a grand home. For the houses of fort-commanders on
Hadrian's Wall are comparable in style and scale with the villas of
the wealthy Romano-British elite. Visitors to museums along the
wall will, for example, be struck by the quality of the jewellery on
display. The detailed carving of some brooches is extraordinary
(fig. 16). Men of lower ranks were forbidden to marry; they should
have no ties to the area, so that they could be rapidly posted
elsewhere. However, whatever the prohibitions, ordinary soldiers

Fig. 17 The tombstone of the doctor Anicius Ingenuus, from
Housesteads

did contract illegal marriages, often keeping wives and families in the *vicus*; some of the jewellery on display may have belonged to such women. By the third and fourth centuries the civilian settlements had, in fact, become prime recruiting grounds for the army; the sons of soldiers frequently choosing to follow their fathers into the army.

Medicine

As well as a highly trained fighting force, the Roman army was also a centre for medical expertise. The Roman army needed medical experts, for both men and animals. Men might be wounded in battle but everyday illnesses and injuries were also a problem. At Vindolanda the tablets make several mentions of veterinary doctors, while inscriptions and the discovery of medical instruments and hospital buildings make it plain that medical care was regularly required. Doctors might take short-term commissions in the army; others held the rank of centurion and made a career out of the army. One such centurion-doctor is recorded on an inscription from Housesteads (fig. 17). The strength report of the Tungrians at Vindolanda is again relevant in this context. It records thirty-one men unfit for service – six wounded, fifteen simply recorded as sick and ten suffering from inflamed eyes. Surgery on eyes was performed in the Roman world: the Roman medical writer Celsus describes an operation on cataracts. Whereas modern cataract surgery removes the cataract from the eye by breaking it up and sucking it out, Celsus uses a technique which breaks the cataract and pushes it away from the iris, out of the line of sight. Tullie House Museum in Carlisle has on display a needle which was used for cataract surgery, together with surgical forceps very similar to their modern equivalents. A collection of instruments at Corbridge includes sounding instruments, probes, scalpel handles, a tongue depressor and a traction hook, none differing much from those used by today's doctors and veterinary surgeons. Techniques may have been more rudimentary but for those who believe the dogma of huge advances in modern science and medicine, these instruments act as a salutary reminder of the advanced state of Roman medical knowledge.

On the veterinary side, the most obvious work would have been the treatment of horses. Without them cavalry was useless; horses had a high value. It is entirely possible that vets also treated the oxen and pigs mentioned in the Vindolanda tablets, as well as other agricultural and domestic animals. However, all the known vets are in the military context of the Vindolanda tablets: Alio, the veterinary doctor, is either owing or owed over ten *denarii*; greetings are sent from Chrauttius to Virilis the vet, via Veldeius, who is a groom of the governor in London. The strong impression is that both vets were military professionals.

Medical care was also available to people in the civilian settlements: inscriptions from Carlisle record the presence of both a pharmacist (*seplesarius*) named Albanus and a Greek doctor called A. Egnatius Pastor. Those who could afford to pay a doctor's fees might also afford a vet to treat their animals. So there may have been civilian vets as well as military ones; we simply lack the evidence.

Chapter 4

Civilian life

Literary and archaeological evidence both tell us a great deal about the military presence on the wall but each has far less to say about the civilian population which lived alongside the army, supplying many of its needs. Roman literary sources are little concerned with native populations in the provinces; when they are mentioned, classical tropes and models distort their presentation. Caesar and Tacitus describe Britons as utterly barbaric, not because they were, but because non-Romans were always represented that way to emphasise the civilised values of Rome (see pp. 19-20 above). Archaeology could potentially tell us much more but its value is limited: archaeologists on the wall have concentrated largely on military sites. There are enough clues to indicate that civilian society there was vibrant and worked in ways slightly different from those in the rest of Roman Britain; but, frustratingly, it is hard to go beyond that. Our picture of life in the civilian settlements of the frontier zone is based on a few examples rather than a wealth of evidence; and it relies to some extent on speculation.

The *vicus*

Study of the *vici* close to the frontier forts provides a typical example of the difficulties involved in discussing civilian life on the wall. Every fort spawned its own *vicus*, a civilian settlement occupied by people who depended for their livelihood on the money provided by the soldiers in the fort. Ideally each *vicus* would have been excavated with as much attention to detail as the fort itself; it would provide a wealth of information about the merchants, shopkeepers and civilians who lived in such close proximity to the soldiers. Yet at almost every fort on the wall the excavators chose not to look beyond the fort walls: soldiers were

interesting; civilians were not. Only the *vici* of Housesteads and
Vindolanda have been excavated in any detail; those at other forts
are known, for the most part, only from aerial photography. We
have to assume that life in all of them was similar; so conclusions
drawn from Housesteads and Vindolanda must serve as generally
applicable to all.

Fig. 18 An aerial view of the fort and *vicus* at Vindolanda

The vast majority of buildings in a *vicus* were what are known
as 'strip houses' – long, thin, rectangular structures (fig. 18).
Those laid out before visitors to Vindolanda are ideal examples;
aerial photography indicates that all *vici* comprised such buildings
(fig. 19). Their size varied but most were large; their floor areas

in many cases exceed fifty square metres. Some served partly as shops. At Housesteads one was constructed with shutters the full length of its street-facing wall; so the entire frontage could effectively be removed, allowing passers-by to view the wares presumably on display within. Vindolanda has a building which bears remarkable similarities to houses at Pompeii; just inside the door opening onto the street was the foundation for an L-shaped

Fig. 19 One of the strip buildings from the *vicus* at Housesteads

counter. In both instances, the front was a shop, the rear living quarters. The fort baths were also situated in the *vicus* and we may, therefore, speculate that civilian residents were permitted to use them. Excavators at Vindolanda have uncovered a single temple to an unknown Romano-Celtic deity; and it would be amazing if others did not await discovery there and in other *vici*. Its presence certainly gives an indication of the wealth of the Vindolanda's *vicus*: temples were by no means cheap to build and represent commitment of significant resources to the project, by an individual or by the community as a whole.

Some residents of the *vicus* were clearly wealthy. Goldsmiths are recorded both by one of the Vindolanda tablets and by a writing tablet from Carlisle. Such men must have been rich themselves, to afford their raw materials, and reliant on a significant number of well-to-do customers to keep them in business. Finds from the *vici* include jewellery and silverware. On a more mundane level,

Fig. 20 The tombstone of the freedwoman Regina, from South Shields

the Vindolanda tablets mention merchants and shopkeepers who sold both local and imported food, alcohol, clothes and footwear.

Some of them must have been local men, though it is clear that not all were. Tombstones the length of Hadrian's Wall give the impression of a very cosmopolitan society. One from South Shields (fig. 20) records Regina, who came from the region of Verulamium (St. Albans); she had come some distance to live in South Shields in a period when few travelled further than their nearest city. Compared to others, however, Regina's move was pretty ordinary. She was the wife and slave of Barates, who came from Palmyra in Syria. Also at South Shields lived a Moorish freedman. Other Syrians are recorded on gravestones from Corbridge, where we also find Diodora, high priestess of the Tyrian (Tyre in modern Lebanon) Hercules. Germans are to be found at Chesters, Carrawburgh and Netherby. Carvoran was home to women from Dalmatia; and a Spaniard lived at Birrens. Given that comparatively few tombstones survive from the northern frontier, this handful of examples must be only the tip of an iceberg; the *vici* were home to people from across the empire. It is worth noting that, while *vicus* residents were in many cases clearly wealthy, they did not spend their money on grand houses, like those of their counterparts elsewhere in Roman Britain. There is little evidence that they advertised their wealth and status – itself a surprising and interesting phenomenon. Wealth, properly displayed, allowed a man to climb society's ladder, gaining social and often administrative rank. If wealth was not on display in ways common throughout the rest of empire, it follows that here there must have been nothing to be achieved from such self aggrandisment.

What attracted these people? Anyone familiar with the Northumbrian winter will realise the shock it must have been for someone used to Syrian sunshine; the attractions of Hadrian's Wall to merchants from the eastern empire are hard to fathom; yet they came in large numbers. The answer has to be money. The wages paid in coin to soldiers meant a lot of disposable income was concentrated on the frontier. That created an instant market and the market attracted merchants, who in turn had money to buy goods from other merchants, so extending the market. Hadrian's Wall offered real opportunities to make money.

The size of *vici* along the wall reflects their economic role.

Given the limited excavation of them, we can only guess at the size of most, though aerial photography gives a fair notion of their extent. Thirty houses are known at Vindolanda; the topography suggests space for another thirty. Chesters and Old Carlisle were probably larger; at the latter buildings followed the main road for half a kilometre and the minor roads were lined with more. All three forts were much the same size; so differences in the extent of their *vici* cannot depend simply on the strength of the garrison. Vindolanda lies somewhat out of the way, at a distance from major Roman roads; larger *vici* were close to major roads and road-junctions.[35] Their merchants had greater opportunities to grow rich, from passing traffic and by redistributing goods transported along the main arteries; simple economics dictate that more people gravitate to places where financial opportunities are better. The Carlisle goldsmith had access to merchants travelling east-west along the Stanegate, as well as north-south by the west-coast route or even by sea; he could sell his wares to more people and had a greater range of merchants with whom to trade than his counterpart at Vindolanda. While soldiers' wages provided the primary impetus for the existence of a *vicus*, its continued growth depended upon access to a wider market than that from the fort alone.

It has been suggested that in the third century the *vici* of Britain generally had rudimentary walls. Wallsend certainly provides evidence of this development. Fifty metres to the west of the fort has been found a bank and ditch of late second- or early third-century date.[36] It represents a change in the way *vicus* communities saw themselves. The walls were not for defence; any suggestion that they were has much to do with the military bias in the wall's archaeological interpretation. A better explanation is that they played the same role as a city's walls. They defined the community, setting its limits in a physical way and, at the same time, making a statement about its wealth and status – that it could *afford* to erect walls. The project would have required agreement from powerful and wealthy residents, along with a probable financial contribution from them. Permission from the garrison-commander in the fort may also have been needed; cities planning the construction of walls required a special grant from the province's civilian authorities. As the cornerstones of civilisation, cities were, of course, administratively very different from villages and *vici* but the basic principal that a community could not itself build walls without permission from the correct authority is a strong one. The correct authority in the case of the *vicus* was the fort's commander.

There are examples where the army played a role in the affairs of the settlement, others where the occupants acted in concert. To begin with, the bath-house of the fort was often, as at Vindolanda, in the *vicus*, facilitating regular contact between soldiers and civilians even when the former had little money to spend. The positioning of the bath-house suggests that the army may well have owned the land on which the settlement was built, that the *vicus*, for all it benefited the soldiers, only developed by permission of the army. It may even imply that the military had an administrative role in the settlement's affairs; in the absence of a police force it must at least have provided law enforcement and justice for the community. That the army owned the land is further borne out by the regularity of the plots on which the buildings stood. A degree of planning can be seen; only someone who owned the land and oversaw the affairs of the *vicus* could enforce this.[37] Given that the army built the wall, the forts and the *Vallum*, that the *Vallum* was broken by the presence of a *vicus*, it seems reasonable to conclude that the army owned the land on which it was built.

That ownership would make an administrative role in the *vicus* natural for the army; it meant that the community effectively owed its very existence to them and that they took on a major role in local civilian affairs. The communities were, nonetheless, permitted some self-government: perhaps one or more army officers might be permanent members of the governing council; or the council might be subject to the fort-commander's authority. From Vindolanda, Carriden and Old Carlisle there are inscriptions which record dedications made by the inhabitants of the *vicus* as a whole, while community decrees are also recorded at Housesteads. So the settlement had a sense of itself as an organised community – something also indicated later on by the construction of a defining wall. In cities communal dedications were organised by the *curia* (the city's governing council); we should probably expect the same in the *vicus*, though the army's presence meant the community was never truly independent. This may explain why rich merchants chose not to advertise their wealth: they could never achieve true administrative rank without moving to the cities of the south; to do so would mean abandoning the source of their wealth.

It has traditionally been thought that the demise of the *vici* along the wall followed raids from the north during the 360s; this explanation suited the common view of Hadrian's Wall as a military frontier – and a more general view of history that considers wars and battles as the key events. Closer examination of the archaeological evidence, however, indicates the error of such an explanation for the decline of the civilian settlements; socio-economic factors were the true cause. The *vicus* at Housesteads contains very little fourth century material – just enough to support the picture of a few remaining residents, not the kind of bustling community found there in the third century. The extensive coin series from Vindolanda dries up in the 270s, suggesting that the *vicus* had ceased effective existence. The two sites together argue for an end in the third century to the civilian settlements in the area – a picture also supported by limited excavation at Wallsend.

These three forts (like all the wall-forts) continued to be occupied until withdrawal from Britain of the Roman military and administrative presence in the early fifth century. The late third-century disappearance of the *vici*, therefore, seems strange. The explanation for it lies in two military changes. As the army was the main reason for the presence of the settlements, any changes to the way it operated would have a direct effect upon them. In the course of the third century military units became smaller; fewer soldiers were stationed in the frontier forts. There was immediately less money circulating in the region. That was compounded by a shift in the way the army was paid: the details are hard to discern but it is thought that during the late third century part at least of soldiers' wages began to be paid in kind rather than cash. Barter would have returned as a norm for economic exchange, making it difficult for merchants to make their living. Coinage represented easily stored and transportable wealth, facilitating economic exchange, especially over long distances; a bag of coins could be sent to southern England or Gaul in exchange for wine or pottery. The equivalent wealth counted in tunics or cattle was not so readily transferable. As smaller and smaller quantities of coin circulated on the wall, fewer and fewer merchants could survive; the *vici* disappeared.[38]

Towns – Carlisle and Corbridge

The role of the city in the Romano-British context can essentially be defined in terms of four areas – administration and politics, economy, religion and entertainment. It was the centre for administration of its own affairs and those of the surrounding area, its magistrates providing leadership much as a local council does today. Law courts were a feature of that, often in a building called a *basilica*. It was there that a man could bring his disputes with his neighbour, tenant or landlord. The *forum* was the formal and informal meeting place for the city's residents, also providing open space for the markets which were the focus for the economic activity of both city and hinterland. There the merchants were based, trading with local farmers eager to exchange their surplus output for small luxuries or the necessities they could not produce themselves. There, too, the elite could buy their luxuries, locally produced or imported from around the empire: fine wines, silks, pottery, jewellery, books – the list is almost endless. The city was also a centre for temples, the focus for religious sacrifices and processions in honour of the gods of the Roman pantheon, including the cult of the emperor himself, as well as the local deities. Finally the city incorporated the theatres, amphitheatre, bars, restaurants and brothels. All these conformed to a Roman model (though they may have been altered over time by British expectations and traditions) and all contributed to the process of 'Romanisation' (see pp. 24-6 below). Essentially that term is commonly used to describe the way in which native populations were assimilated into the empire. Roman modes of dress, housing, diet, ornamentation and even the use of the Latin language – and the British elite may have had libraries of Latin works – came to be associated with social standing. Following the example of Roman administrators from Italy who came in the wake of the army, Britons with money built stone villas and town-houses in a Mediterranean style. They gave their wives jewellery which imitated (or was even bought from the same source as) that of the administrators' wives. They imported Falerian wine from the Italian Campania and beautifully decorated and glazed Samian pottery from Gaul. They behaved as Roman noblemen, so that the administrators who held power in Britain in the first century AD treated them as equals and allowed them a share in that power. Very swiftly Britain's social elite became indistinguishable from their Mediterranean counterparts; when excavating a villa, it is impossible to tell whether its owner was ethnically Italian, from elsewhere in the empire or a Briton. To seek ethnic origins is, in fact, to ask the wrong question: the process of Romanisation meant everyone in the empire, at least at the top of the social hierarchy, was a Roman. Indeed in AD 212 almost everyone became a Roman citizen, making questions of ethnicity even less relevant.

The cities, in a network across Britain, were a focus for this Romano-British elite to show off their power and wealth. Power in one's own local city, whether in Britain or elsewhere, might lead ultimately to power within the province, promotion to senatorial status, even a move to Rome. Success in one's city could be the basis of a high-powered political career for oneself or one's descendants. As an example of this in action, the fourth-century poet Ausonius was a member of the elite class of Bordeaux (*Burdigala*) and rose to become consul in Rome.

Roman ideology maintained that, if a man was rich and powerful, he also had a duty to serve his local city. This he could do by spending money on feasts and festivals for the inhabitants; in return he would be rewarded with a public inscription or statue recording his generosity (visitors to Pompeii, for instance, encounter many inscriptions of this kind). Otherwise he could provide civic buildings or pay for their upkeep; at Pompeii even the official weights and measures used in economic transactions bear an inscription in honour of the man who donated them. British cities worked on the same basis. Lastly the Romano-British nobleman could hold priesthoods and magistracies within the city. As head priest of the local cult of Jupiter or the cult of the deified emperor; he might sit on the city's governing body (*curia*) or take responsibility for hearing cases in its law court. Like anyone with influence, he would be courted by clients, people from lower down the social scale, hoping to obtain favours from their patron and offering in return their political allegiance. They would visit him at his town-house every morning when he was in residence; when he was not, they might attend his villa in the countryside. The elite were thus a focus that drew people to the city to spend money; patron and client alike were the main source of the money which allowed city merchants to continue trading. It was the elite who shaped the city. Their houses there and their villas on the rural estates provided and demonstrated their wealth and power within the Roman system.

Society on the northern frontier, however, did not function in quite the same way. Around Gloucester, for example, were the Roman cities of Gloucester itself, Cirencester and Caerwent. Not so far away was Silchester and, a little beyond, Winchester to the south, St Albans and London to the north-west. The roads between passed through many smaller towns. On Hadrian's Wall there was no similar network of settlements. Neither of the towns of Carlisle and Corbridge was surrounded by a network of villas. Roman society, defined elsewhere by its cities and their respective hinterlands, simply did not work in the wall area as it did in almost the whole of the empire.

Both Carlisle and Corbridge began life in the later first century AD as *vici*; they expanded during the next two centuries to become towns – a development almost certainly officially recognised. At Carlisle the fort continued to be manned throughout the Roman occupation of Britain; at Corbridge, on the other hand, the fort was abandoned, perhaps in the 170s AD, though the army continued to maintain a significant presence there. The initial existence of both sites owed more to economic factors than to the Roman authorities' desire to have civilian settlements in the region disseminating the values of Roman civilisation. This attitude was a continuing feature of Carlisle's history; by the third century the settlement had grown from a *vicus* into a flourishing community covering around seventy-four acres. While the richest families of other urban communities in Roman Britain derived their wealth from agriculture, the richest in Carlisle were traders. This was unusual; for Rome's social ideology normally precluded the social elite from trade: the only respectable way they could make money was by farming. The tombstones from Carlisle's cemeteries record an extensive populace of wealthy traders, as in the *vici*, and their wealth is seen in the quality of sculpture of those monuments.

Few large houses are known from Carlisle but in three that have been excavated the wealth of the occupants is evident. The first (on the Lanes site) began life as successor to a military building. In the mid-second century a timber house with three separate ranges was constructed. That was followed during the third century by a stone building, perhaps with a second range of buildings; and later in the third century the original house was extended to both east and west, one room being given a hypocaust. That was an expensive feature, usually interpreted (along with painted wall plaster and mosaic floors) as a distinct sign of wealth. The house was surrounded by yards, unusual in a Romano-British town-house; they possibly had some function associated with trade – unloading and storage of goods or corralling of animals. There was another hypocausted building in Scotch Street; and parts of an extremely large stone structure have been discovered lying partly beneath the Tullie House Museum. This was at least fifty-three metres long, its walls covered with high quality white plaster. It seems too large to have been a private house; rather it should be seen as a public building, the only one known in Carlisle – perhaps the *forum*, the *basilica* or even the town's bathhouse. Not enough of its structure

Fig. 21 The remains of the aqueduct and fountain from Corbridge

has been uncovered to allow more definite identification. Its sheer size, however, indicates that Carlisle was rich enough to afford large, impressive buildings.

It is tempting to say, on the evidence of the two houses known, that Carlisle's social elite chose not to spend their money on great displays of wealth. Each house had only a single hypocausted room; neither produced evidence of mosaic floors. The occupants of both buildings were certainly reasonably well-to-do, since they did not live in strip houses of the type found in the *vici* and found at Blackfriars Street and St. Mary's Gate in Carlisle. As has been pointed out, however, in the *vici* even rich merchants lived in strip houses; wealth on the northern frontier was not shown in grand houses like those in the rest of Roman Britain. Reliable conclusions about the situation in Carlisle cannot be drawn from just two stone-built houses but our knowledge of towns in the rest of Roman Britain may show how different society was in the frontier zone.

Little more is known of Carlisle's development from *vicus* to urban settlement or of its history into the fifth century and beyond. Excavation beneath any modern city is difficult; for homes and businesses cannot be dismantled to allow archaeological exploration. More is known about Corbridge, though only part of the town has been excavated. The problem there is that the excavators have concentrated on military rather than civilian aspects of the site. So much more is known about the military store houses and workshops of the third century than about development of the civilian community.

By the third century Corbridge had not expanded to the same extent as Carlisle; its area was around forty acres, a little more than half the size of Carlisle. There is no evidence of the grand houses occupied by a social elite; instead a number of strip houses are known. As the *vici* of the wall show, rich merchants might live in such houses; in the frontier zone wealth and status were not displayed in the expected ways. There is, however, more evidence at Corbridge than at Carlisle for community spending. A small aqueduct carried water to a tank on the main street, originally part of an ornate fountain-house (figs 21 and 22). Beyond this, down the town's main street, lies an open patch of ground, which once comprised a courtyard enclosed by four wings. Its function has been the subject of debate: it may have been a storehouse, though its shape makes it look very much like a *forum*. A clear date might make discussion easier but the evidence is simply not available. A 'best guess' would be that it was begun in the late 160s or 170s, about the time the fort was abandoned. Corbridge's role as a town – an administrative and economic centre – suggests that a *forum*

Fig. 22 The Lion from the fountainhead at Corbridge

should be expected. However, it was clearly unfinished; perhaps the town ran out of money during the third century. The demise of the *vici* seems to indicate that the northern frontier underwent economic impoverishment at that time. That for much of its history the inhabitants of Corbridge were wealthy is shown by the coinage record. Around eight thousand coins derive from the site – more than from any other site in the north of Roman Britain, even including the provincial capital and legionary base at York.

Corbridge and Carlisle provide evidence for military presence throughout their history. Corbridge was home to a number of legionaries, who ran the workshops and the stores (see p. 51 above). Here (and at Carlisle) separate walled enclosures were built to house these activities and most of the impressive structures to be seen at Corbridge today are the remains of those. The well-preserved third-century granary (fig. 8) was also for military, rather than civilian, use; its size suggests that, as at South Shields, the army kept the town as a key point for the distribution of supplies to the wall-forts. The presence of legionaries certainly suggests that the workshops at Corbridge were intended to supply goods along the entire wall; for legionaries were specialists in such activities and Corbridge had by the third century become a key part of the frontier zone's supply network.

An important feature of any city was its wall, a sacred boundary symbolically dividing urban civilisation from the barbaric country-side (see pp. 24-7 above). Corbridge, though not in Roman legal terms a city, nonetheless had a wall. A pottery *mortarium* (used for grinding grain), sealed beneath the wall, gives an earliest possible date for its construction *ca* AD 130. Such items could, of course, have remained in use for some time, even lain in the ground for a while before the wall was built; so all the *mortarium* tells us is that the wall could not have been built before 130. In fact a third-century context for its construction is far more likely, since it was then that many of Britain's cities and smaller towns received walls.

Roman ideology suggests that Carlisle, too, should have had walls but no trace of them has yet been found. Scholars argue that they must have existed because in the Venerable Bede's *Life of St Cuthbert* (written in the eighth century), the saint is said to have visited Carlisle and seen walls. His visit took place in the seventh century and it has been proposed that even then Carlisle was still functioning as a city – or at least that its ruins were still visible. That no city wall has yet been found is not an insuperable difficulty; Carlisle has not been comprehensively excavated; its walls may await discovery. A more serious problem is the nature of our source: Bede was not an eye-witness to the life of St Cuthbert (he wrote a century later) and he cannot, therefore, have been working from first-hand evidence. He was writing not history but hagiography; a genre in which he was not bound to relate fact, even if he knew it. St Cuthbert's life was to be held up as an ideal, an example for good Christians to follow. There need be no real truth behind it at all. Bede knew that, in general, ruined Roman cities had walls and he included that detail at Carlisle to give his narrative added credibility. In this lies our best hope of uncovering some truth about Carlisle's walls. Bede wrote in Jarrow (now part of Newcastle); the nearest Roman city to him was Carlisle; so it is likely that his knowledge of ruined Roman cities was based on Carlisle. Whether St. Cuthbert went there and saw walls or not is unimportant; but by throwing in this detail, Bede is telling us that he knew the city had walls. The conclusion must be that they were still visible in the eighth century.

The legal status of a settlement was important; for it dictated such things as residents' liability to pay taxes. We do not know the legal status of Corbridge; its third-century walls are typical of small, Romano-British towns of the period; they need not indicate city status. At Carlisle we have enough evidence at least to specu-late that it was a *civitas*, that it had the legal status of a city: two inscriptions from Roman Britain mention a *civitas Carvetiorum*, or city governing the territory of a tribe called the Carvetii. The tribe is known to have lived in northern Britain. A milestone found on Hadrian's Wall measures distance from the *civitas Carvetiorum*. Carlisle was the largest settlement in the region and has the best evidence of significant civilian wealth; it is hard to see anywhere else as *civitas Carvetiorum*. The date when she was granted her city-status is unknown. The milestone cannot be dated earlier than AD 258 but that only means that it was put in place in the second half of the third century. A single milestone cannot date the grant of city-status.

To some extent the question whether Corbridge and Carlisle deserve to be termed cities is irrelevant. 'City' is in any case an inexact translation for *civitas*, *municipium* and *colonia* (which Romans used for their three most socially significant settlement types), since it is loaded with modern resonances which hardly applied in the ancient world. 'City' in the Roman context is effectively shorthand for a settlement with social, economic and religious significance within a large area. We cannot be absolutely certain of the legal status of Carlisle. That of Corbridge is unknown. Both clearly had social, economic and religious importance in their regions. However they hardly matched the model of a Roman city outlined above; because they differed from the norm in the crucial areas of governance and in the role played by their social elite.

The case has been made that the army had a key role in ruling the *vicus* communities of the frontier. Similar reasoning may be applied to the larger communities of Corbridge and Carlisle. Both, after all, began their life as *vici*, subject to military government from the start. The land on which they were built was owned by the military and that marked them as different from cities in the rest of Britain, which were carefully founded as independent communities according to set rules. The *vici* were never independent and we should expect the same to have been true of Carlisle and Corbridge. What little we know of both suggests the continuation of a strong military presence and that was in itself quite alien to the concept of a city as a civilian, non-military community. As in the case of the *vici*, it seems reasonable to conclude that the army replaced the social elite in controlling the frontier's urban communities, dominating society in the region of the wall. An elite still governed the 'city' but it was one that depended for its status on military rank rather than wealth, private benefactions and consequent social standing.

Rural life

Archaeological exploration of the countryside in the frontier zone has not been systematic but we can still form a reasonable picture of occupation patterns in the region immediately north of the wall. Aerial photography has shown that the area was extensively occupied. In the Eden Valley and the Solway Plain hundreds of farmsteads have been mapped in this way. Population was particularly dense in the Cumberland sea plain just north of Carlisle, where there is evidence for numbers of stone-built farmhouses, like that at Ewe Close. Sadly this picture is not replicated south of the wall. Native farmsteads have traditionally been regarded as alien to 'true' Roman society – not a necessary part of 'Roman' archaeology; it is only north of the wall where archaeologists have not been so constrained by misleading labels, that useful work on the countryside has been done.

South of the wall, archaeologists have for much of the nineteenth and twentieth centuries merely noted an absence of villas. That absence is in itself interesting because it throws light on the appearance and behaviour of the social elite in the frontier zone. The apparent absence – or at least archaeological invisibility – of a ruling elite, noted in the *vici* and the towns, is replicated in the countryside. One would expect to find a network of villas in the region of a Roman city; social ideology expected the elite to own both town and country houses; both showed a man's wealth and status. For a villa was more than a farm; it was the centre of his country property; from it he ran the estate, which was the source of his wealth. Agricultural estate was his only 'proper' source of wealth. The typical villa consisted of ranges of houses situated around a courtyard. At these sites archaeologists typically find evidence of considerable wealth – floors heated by hypocausts, fine mosaics, walls plastered and painted in a range of colours or even with fresco-pictures; and the artefacts including fine pottery, glassware and coinage.

Along Hadrian's Wall, however, farmsteads are just that – farmsteads. They are not built in the form of villas and they show no evidence of wealth. Either the social elite were not present or they chose not to show their wealth in their country properties. The former seems unlikely, because St Patrick tells us in his *Letter to the Soldiers of Coroticus* (probably written in the mid-fifth century) that his father was a decurion and lived in a place called Bannavem Taberniae. The name is often associated with Birdoswald, which became a civilian settlement in the fifth century (see pp. 97-9 below). Decurions – the 'curial classes' – ranked as the highest social group and held responsibility for the governance of cities. If such a position survived the end of Roman rule, then it must have had even greater relevance under it; from Patrick's writings we see that a social elite existed on Hadrian's Wall but the fact was that they simply did not behave like the elite in the rest of Britain: they did not show off their wealth in country homes.

Farmers did not experience huge changes in their lifestyle as a result of the army's presence, though some changed their homes from the typical round-houses of iron-age Britain to rectangular buildings more in keeping with Roman architectural style (fig. 23). This may have been in imitation of buildings in the *vici*. It is strange that there is so little evidence of wealth in

Fig. 23 A Romano-British farmer beside his round-house

the countryside around the southern side of the frontier, despite the evident wealth of the *vici*. Excavation of the Cumberland Infirmary site in Carlisle, just a kilometre or so northwest of the Roman town, has uncovered a settlement – it might loosely be termed a village – consisting of a group of round-houses, first century in date, which were replaced in the second by rectangular buildings. Hardly any material goods of any quality were found there: either the inhabitants were not wealthy or they chose not to follow the pattern, common to the rest of Roman Britain, of showing their wealth in their property. Given that local farmers must have been first port of call for those supplying the frontier army – why transport goods long distances at great cost when they are available locally? – it would seem strange if wealth did not trickle down to them. Maybe they paid their taxes in kind and so received no payment for their produce. Perhaps they chose to spend their wealth on more livestock and land rather than prestige goods. This sort of explanation would fit with the absence of villa-type buildings despite the presence of a recognisable social elite. It all adds up to the picture of a society operating here not quite as expected in the rest of Roman Britain.

Romanisation

The evidence for what might, in traditional terms, be called the 'Romanisation' of the frontier zone is generally not strong. There were no villas and only two settlements of any size, at both of which there has to be some doubt how far local elite were allowed self-governance free from military control. The local countryside shows almost no sign of any wealth. The frontier people were not, in other words, living in quite the same sort of society as those further south. Were they less Romanised – less 'civilised'? Or does it indicate that the army was so overwhelming a presence that the local population never moved forward from beneath its shadow?

Before answering those questions, it is worth asking whether 'Romanisation' is a useful term to describe the process by which Britain was assimilated into the Roman empire. It was coined by Francis Haverfield, the first professional specialist in Romano-British archaeology (he had revised a standard edition of Virgil beforehand) when he was appointed to an academic post in the University of Oxford in 1892. Scholarly trends at the time saw Romans as bringing a vastly superior culture to Britain, civilising the island (see ch. 6 below).[39] So, when Haverfield used the term 'Romanisation', he saw a process which went only one way: the Romans gave their civilisation to a backward society, so aiding British social and cultural development. For him the history of Britain was a series of improvements leading toward an ideal society – an approach underpinned by the assumption that, not only was Roman culture more 'advanced' than that of iron-age Britain, but that nineteenth- and twentieth-century British culture was itself more advanced than that of the Roman empire. In the analysis of societies such vague, sweeping value-judgements may be tempting but they tend to mask details and nuances. To claim Roman civilisation was superior to – or more 'advanced' than – British culture is just such a judgement. As such it obscures the strong values of the pre-existing iron-age society. If we use the term 'Romanisation', we should employ it in the sense of a two-way process, the coming together of two distinctive cultures; if the term cannot be divorced from notions of Roman cultural superiority, then it should be abandoned.

To see the area around Hadrian's Wall as less civilised than other areas of Roman Britain is to set the debate on a false trail. Society operated differently in the northern frontier zone and the simple statement that it was less 'Romanised' (implying 'less civilised') represents a misjudgement of the way it functioned. The strongest explanation for the operation of the region's society is that the dominant influence was not a Romano-British city elite but the Roman army. That changed the way society was ordered. Power resided with military officers, not civilian leaders; it was gained and exercised in a different way. In York, Wroxeter, Cirencester or any city elsewhere in Britain, men gained power by spending money conspicuously, thus attracting political support. They owned fine houses in the city and the countryside, demonstrating their social status; their power, once they had amassed political support, was exercised through a series of magistracies in the city they controlled. At Carlisle and Corbridge (as in the *vici*) these opportunities did not exist because the army seems to have maintained control; the top political strata were closed to local elites. Social matters in the frontier zone were ordered differently, as reflected in the archaeological record: men did not spend money conspicuously to achieve political success; for such success was simply not forth-coming in an area under such heavy military control. Hence the absence of the usual trappings of Romano-British wealth.

Chapter 5

Hadrian's Wall
and the end of Roman Britain

Books on Roman Britain, and Hadrian's Wall in particular, usually separate analysis of the late Roman period (and the centuries thereafter) from discussion of earlier periods. This is partly an accident of scholarship. The 'late' Roman period is somewhat arbitrarily regarded as beginning in the late third century with the reign of Diocletian (AD 284-305). Its conclusion is much debated: it might end with the sack of Rome by Alaric's Goths in AD 410; with the abdication in 476 of Romulus Augustulus, the last Roman emperor in the west (emperors, of course, long continued to rule in the eastern, Byzantine, half of the empire); or with the development, during the later fifth and sixth centuries, of the Germanic kingdoms in the former western provinces of the empire.[40] It is thought of as a period apart – now usually termed 'late antiquity', especially since the publication of Peter Brown's *The World of Late Antiquity* (1971) – and it is studied largely in isolation from the rest of imperial history. This is, on the one hand, a good thing for our view of Roman history as a whole; for it ensures that the period is seen as important and interesting in itself, standing mid-way between Roman imperialism and the mediaeval world, not just a decaying aftermath to Rome's glory-days. It can, on the other hand, give a false impression; for it may suggest to the unwary that the earlier centuries can be judged as a unity, that changes in the way the empire functioned occurred only at the end of the third century. Separation of the two periods also emphasises the *end* of Rome, so that fourth-, fifth- and (in provinces other than Britain) sixth-century evidence is inevitably often interpreted in light only of that end, whatever event one accepts as signalling it. Late antique developments are thus seen only in terms of progression towards final disintegration.

This is a particular problem in Britain, where the late Roman period is shorter than in other provinces. For the army and provincial administration seem to have been withdrawn early in the fifth century, leaving an interregnum traditionally presented as a period of constant warfare between rampaging Saxons and the residue of the remaining Romano-British. The end is reflected in the stone-built cities and villas, which had mostly collapsed into ruin by about the mid-fifth century; so obvious an end draws the minds of scholars to see the fourth century as no more than a steady decline towards that calamity.

This approach, with its focus on collapse, rather precludes consideration of a population trying to adapt to fifth-century pressures, restructuring their society in the sudden absence of government so long imposed from afar. Yet that is precisely what can be observed in the region of Hadrian's Wall during the fifth and sixth centuries, the period often called 'sub-Roman'. To discuss the region in late and sub-Roman times as something quite distinct from the earlier periods has certain drawbacks, though it does allow developments during the fourth and fifth centuries to be seen as a whole.

There are, too, some problems in dealing with the archaeological remains of the period. The first arises from nineteenth – and, to a certain extent, twentieth-century archaeological practice. Only quite recently have historians and archaeologists begun to see late antiquity as interesting and worth detailed study. Until the mid-twentieth century the later Roman empire was thought decadent and 'inferior' to earlier periods: on archaeological sites late and sub-Roman levels were regularly ignored; all too often they were dug through to admit excavators to the 'real Roman' levels beneath.[41] On many older sites evidence for the fifth and sometimes even fourth centuries is missing.

A second problem is that, even where we have late and sub-Roman material, it remains very difficult to date. Precise chronology in earlier periods is derived from coinage and from pottery types common to a whole province or even larger parts of the empire. The last coin-issues reached Britain in the early fifth century; and they are rare. Imported pottery largely ceased to arrive in Britain about the same time and even the more ubiquitous British potteries shut down; there remained only locally made wares for which there are no dateable typologies. It is still possible to say that one level precedes another but neither can be given absolute dates. And, while it is usually said that coins might last in circulation for about thirty years under normal conditions, in the abnormal conditions of the fifth century one suspects that they circulated far longer. They would need to in a cash-economy like that in the area of Hadrian's Wall, if the economy were not to collapse. A clue to the length of time coins circulated lies in the extent of wear on those found but that is highly subjective. Firm dates are hard to come by in the fifth century; so historians and archaeologists tend to construct wildly differing chronologies.[42]

Barbarian invasions (?)

Gildas, a monk who wrote, in the mid-sixth century, the *De Excidio Britonum* (*On the Ruin of Britain*) – our only relatively contemporary account of the end of Roman Britain – provides an overview of the final phase of Hadrian's Wall and a chronological framework for fourth- and fifth-century events. In the preface to what is effectively a long sermon on the evils of sixth-century Britain, he gives a history of Britain by way of explaining how the country reached what he saw as its present parlous state. He represents Britain under Roman rule as largely Christian – thus peaceful and happy. The late third century persecution of Christians under Diocletian he mentions as a great evil but one which had no more than a temporary impact. After that his narrative becomes far more detailed but far more confused. He claims that the Antonine Wall was built by legions which came to Britain in the wake of rebellion by the British general Maximus in the 380s; that Hadrian's Wall itself was a response to invasions by Picts and Irish in the subsequent period.

In Gildas' account, the construction of the wall was Rome's final involvement in Britain. He presents the Romans as an external force, governing Britain from afar. After the Romans built the wall, they withdrew, intending never to return. The British meanwhile manned the wall but were swiftly over-run by invading Picts and Irish. The wall and the northern towns were abandoned. This was only the prelude to worse evils: the Saxons, arriving in the mid-fifth century, destroyed Roman Britain and Gildas presents their invasion in the bloodiest terms: walls and towers were destroyed; bodies hacked to pieces, to be eaten by birds and beasts; and the quantity of blood spilled is compared to the outflow of a winepress.

Gildas' efficacy as a source for late Roman Britain is, therefore, extremely limited. His grasp of basic chronology is poor, witness his fourth-century attribution of both frontier walls. Nor were the cities so dramatically destroyed as he maintains; they were abandoned and in ruins before the first Saxons set foot on the south coast. Yet Gildas may have had access to some source material, which he either misunderstood or misused; his account of the Picts and Irish attacking Britain bears similarities to the description of a 'barbarian conspiracy' in the work of the fourth-century historian Ammianus Marcellinus. According to Ammianus it was in AD 367 that the Saxons of the continent, along with Picts, other Scottish peoples and the Irish, mounted a simultaneous attack on Britain, causing great devastation. If we assume that Gildas had confused Maximus' rebellion of the 380s with that of Magnentius in the 350s, then we may argue that he used Ammianus as a source for fourth-century Britain. This still does not mean there is much truth behind his account. For there is no more archaeological support for Ammianus' story than for that of Gildas. If there was an invasion, then it has left no material trace.

Gildas was, of course, not concerned with writing 'history' in the sense of recording fact. He has far more in common as a writer with the Christian hagiographers and sermon-writers of late antique Gaul than with Roman historians. He wrote with the predominant belief that the people of sixth-century Britain had turned from God; his aim was to bring them back. So he presented the island's past as a series of divine punishments. His warning is clear: if Britain does not become truly Christian (as he defines that), then it can expect to be punished again. That barbarians are God's tool to punish the wicked is a commonplace of Christian writing in late antiquity, one with biblical roots. Gildas' account of the destruction of British cities draws on that of Sodom and Gomorrah, of Gaza and many other cities.[43] In Gildas' eyes, God punishes the wicked, using in Britain the barbarians rather than fire and brimstone; cause and the effect remain the same.

So, when considering Hadrian's Wall during the fourth and fifth centuries, it is best to forget the notion of barbarian invasions. There is no archaeological evidence for them; Gildas' account was not history but a sermon.

The army

A more considered analysis of the end of Hadrian's Wall should begin with the army, since military presence was so integral to the frontier zone. The evidence from the fourth century for shifts in the administration of the forts and of the army is plentiful. Real changes to the Roman army as a whole began with Diocletian in the late third century. He recognised that the organisation of the army and the disposition of units on the frontiers meant that it was improperly prepared to cope with the increased threat from raids into the empire on the Rhine and Danube frontiers. He therefore instituted changes and his reorganisation was continued by Constantine in the early fourth century. Essentially, the frontier army was reduced in strength and in status: its garrisons became known as *limitanei* (frontiersmen). Meantime new field armies were created under the name *comitatenses* (the name is a development of the term *comitatus* or 'company', given for the first time to the emperor's bodyguard and then coming during the third century to mean the imperial headquarters); soldiers in *comitatenses* were paid at a higher rate and given greater privileges. In theory the old distinctions between auxiliary and legionary were swept away; the chief difference between them – the citizenship – had in any case become meaningless when the emperor Caracalla extended that status to everyone within the empire (AD 212). In practice, however, at least as far as Roman Britain was concerned, not much had changed. Some units garrisoned Hadrian's Wall; others were still stationed in the various forts around the rest of the country. The only real difference was that the British legions lost their greater standing and were now on a par with the auxiliary units. All were still trained to a high standard; throughout the empire at this period the difference between soldiers in field armies and those in frontier armies was purely one of staus, not of training and equipment. Real discrepancies between them only started to appear later in the fifth century as the Roman army as a whole began to rely on Germanic mercenaries; they do not apply to Roman Britain.

How did these changes affect the army on Hadrian's Wall? It used commonly to be suggested that a new types of barracks – 'chalets', giving more space to apparently fewer men – were built in the fourth century. Recent excavations have, however, shown that, while such buildings *were* constructed as late as that, they had initially been introduced as early as the first half of the third century. So, on the basis of space available in the barracks, units stationed on the wall were smaller in the fourth than in the second century but the change went back to the third. Thus the army stationed on Hadrian's Wall had shrunk; but this was nothing to do with Diocletian's reforms. Quite possibly, once Caracalla had made everyone a citizen, the attraction of becoming an auxiliary soldier – the opportunity to gain citizenship for one's family along with the attendant benefits that brought – was lost and recruitment suffered.

Inscriptional evidence disappears in the fourth century, so that the forts themselves provide no records of the units occupying them. We should expect that, in accordance with the changes made elsewhere by Diocletian and Constantine, the units were somehow different. However the *Notitia Dignitatum* (or 'List of Offices') suggests otherwise. This document provides a list of administrative officials, military officers and military units, together with the places where they were stationed; its entries date between the end of the fourth century and the mid-fifth. It is argued that they give a reasonably accurate picture of late military dispositions in Britain. The *Notitia* tells us that the units stationed on the wall in the fourth century were largely the same as those shown from inscriptions to have been present during the third. There is no reason, however, to think that Britain entirely avoided the military reorganisation taking place in the rest of the empire. The obvious conclusion is that units kept the same title as they had held before but were assigned to a different role in the overall work of the army. It should be noted that Britain contained no force that could be described as a field army; the nearest were in Gaul, where the threat of Germanic invasions was far greater. Technically, therefore, both legions and auxiliary cohorts had become part of the *limitanei*. That the success of Constantine and the victories of the usurpers Magnentius and

Maximus were based upon the strength of the army stationed in Britain simply reinforces the impression that there was no real difference in the fourth and early fifth centuries between *limitanei* and *comitatenses*. The absence from Britain of an army with the higher status, however, suggests that, as far as the emperors were concerned, the island was of secondary importance.

There are still questions about smaller units and of the 'chalet-style' barracks which appeared in the first half of the third century before the major military reorganisation. It was in part that reorganisation which left units smaller than before. But it has to be added that the army on the wall was in a pretty ramshackle state in the later third century. The continuing presence of the same units throughout the third century is probably confirmed by their mention in the *Notitia Dignitatum* but, at the same time, the archaeological record shows significant levels of disrepair at forts such as Halton Chesters, Rudchester and Birdoswald. At the first two, for example, third-century buildings had fallen down and become covered with earth, indicating disuse of the site, prior to repair and construction of new buildings. At Birdoswald an inscription which dates to the very end of the third century records the rebuilding of the commander's house and the repairs to both headquarters building and bath-house. The obvious conclusion might be that units had become so small during the course of the third century that they did not need to occupy the whole fort, allowing parts of it to fall into disrepair. Obvious though that explanation may be, however, it may not be the best one.

The poor state of important buildings at Birdoswald is in itself interesting. The collapse of the commander's house suggests that either the commander lived in the barracks or he was absent for some reason. The state of this building, of the bath house and of the headquarters building (*praetorium*) – the biggest, grandest and most expensive buildings in the fort – certainly implies a lack of concern for units stationed on the wall, for the very fabric of the forts they manned. The answer may lie not simply with the army itself; for the cities of Britain had also became tatty and rundown in the later third century. The province was impoverished; neither the army nor private individuals had money to spend. The empire as a whole was suffering an economic crisis, including rampant inflation; the coinage increasingly lost its precious metal content and so became devalued. Prices soared; Diocletian's famous 'Edict of Maximum Prices', published across the empire in AD 301, was an attempt to deal with this situation by giving goods fixed values. The army, reliant as it was upon cash, was directly affected. Lack of money for repairs led to the disrepair for which archaeology gives clear evidence. Reforms in the early fourth century, however, seem to have put the wall and its forts into better repair; and they were manned by full-strength units, albeit officially smaller than before.

The army remained on Hadrian's Wall until the complete withdrawal of the Roman military and administrative machine in the early fifth century. There are difficulties with dating that major development precisely. The latest bronze coinage found in Britain dates to AD 402; the 404 issue of bronze coinage known to have taken place in the rest of the empire failed to reach Britain. The very latest *gold* coins are those of Constantius III (AD 407-11), the emperor who, under the now convoluted imperial structure, had responsibility for Britain. As the army was the chief destination for coinage, the absence of this coinage implies that by 411 (at the latest) the army was gone. Our sources record rebellion in Britain in 409 and just a year later a letter written by the emperor Honorius told the British to take responsibility for their own defence. If the evidence provided by our source could be accepted, the province of Britain was cast loose from the empire in 410. The problem is that for events of 409-10 our sources are not reliable. The main one is Zosimus, hardly trustworthy as he wrote at the end of the fifth century; and it can be shown that his account of events in Gaul during the same period contains mistakes. Our evidence for Honorius' letter of 410 is in a chapter discussing events in Italy, so that it makes good sense to accept that a copyist of Zosimus' manuscript misread *Brettia* (Bruttium in southern Italy) and substituted *Brettania* (Britain).[44] So we cannot be absolutely certain of the events leading to withdrawal of the Roman army and administration from Britain or the date at which it took place. It is best to assume that sometime around 410, the army was gone from Britain and from Hadrian's Wall.

The key question is how far withdrawal of the army and the machinery of Roman administration made a difference to everyday life in Britain. It is a very difficult question but one especially pertinent to the northern frontier in the fifth century; for so much of everyday life in the area revolved around the army. The general picture of Britain after 410 is one of rapid decay in the Romanised way of life. By around 450 – though the dating is contentious and varies from site to site – the villas and towns had fallen into disrepair. The army's withdrawal also meant that the character of the northern frontier underwent marked change during the fifth century.

Civilian life

Towards the end of the third century, Diocletian had reorganised the provinces of Britain, sub-dividing the existing two into four – a change which had a general impact on the northern frontier and perhaps on Carlisle in particular. We cannot move much beyond speculation on this because we do not fully understand Diocletian's reorganisation of the provinces; we don't know, crucially, which cities were provincial capitals. It would seem natural that London and York kept their status, giving Britain provinces in the north east and the south east. For the south west the obvious guess is Cirencester, given its size and evident wealth. Caerleon must be discounted; while it was important as a legionary base, it had no standing in civilian life. In the north west Wroxeter and Chester are possibilities, given their proximity to north Wales; Carlisle is another. North Wales had never taken on much in the way of Roman culture; Carlisle, on the other hand, was on the heavily occupied northern frontier, a key part of Roman Britain. On geographical grounds at least, she must be a good candidate for one of the new provincial capitals. To support that argument we need ideally some epigraphic evidence but none is forthcoming; alternatively archaeological evidence, perhaps new building work like the enlargement of the *forum* at Cirencester, would be helpful but again it is lacking. Promotion for Carlisle remains a possibility; it cannot be proven.

Excavation of late Roman Carlisle has simply not been extensive enough to provide more information. At Corbridge the history of excavation is different but the end result (for the fourth and fifth centuries) remains the same as at Carlisle. Early twentieth-century excavations there simply removed the late levels, leaving us ignorant of fourth- and fifth-century developments. However, some of the wall-forts give a glimpse of civilian life after military withdrawal.

The army's departure from the area of the wall was not the end of occupation in the frontier forts. They were originally military structures but, once the army left, history of the sites is best considered in the civilian context. Civilian power structures had hitherto depended on the army (see ch. 4 above); its withdrawal left a power vacuum – one which was, as the subsequent history of the forts shows, rapidly filled.

Fifth-century developments can be discussed in the case of only a few forts because of the limitations of our archaeological evidence. Most of the others may have undergone similar changes, though we cannot tell; it is difficult to believe that only a handful of forts conformed to the pattern of those where evidence exists. At Housesteads – and probably at Birdoswald and Vindolanda, though the evidence there is not as clear cut – the fort walls were encased in banks of earth, presumably because the loss of military (especially legionary) building techniques meant the walls could no longer be repaired when they decayed. However, the very fact that attention was paid to the walls in this way shows they were still felt significant; timber towers were also set into the earth banks at Housesteads, perhaps indicating that the forts continued to have a military function in the fifth century.[45] That is a possible conclusion but again it is one shaped by concentration – to the exclusion of much else – on the wall's military aspects. Given the withdrawal of the army a better analogy might be city walls, which had no defensive function. One role of the city wall was to make a statement about the wealth and status of the place; a wealthy city could afford grand walls. Walls in the northern frontier zone of the fifth century, should probably be seen in the same light. Those responsible for their reconstruction commanded sufficient power and resources to command and finance the work. This is not to say that the new walls were indefensible, simply that defence was not their primary purpose; rather they represented the power and wealth of an individual or the community.

This suggests that post-Roman society on the wall remained focussed on the forts just as it had been in earlier centuries. Just who was based in the forts and commanding the building work, we do not know. What is clear, however, is that wealthy and powerful individuals or groups were carving out areas of responsibility – small kingdoms, perhaps – in the power vacuum left by Roman military withdrawal. It is a situation which has parallels elsewhere in Britain; in south Wales and south-west England, for instance, iron-age hill-forts were reoccupied in the early sixth century. On the frontier transition from Roman military to native civilian administration seems to have been relatively smooth; for in the few cases where detailed archaeological work has been done there appears to have been no period when the forts were completely abandoned, a circumstance which suggests that they were thought ideal places from which to rule, because the lives of the local population already revolved around them. Even so it would be wrong to see them turning into fortified villages. Common sense suggests that the local population still had to eat; so farmers cannot have quit their fields to move into a fort. In any case, on sites where the evidence allows discussion, there is no sign of the small houses one would expect if the local population had moved in.

Birdoswald, where recent work has given a clearer picture of sub-Roman developments, fleshes out the picture. Excavation of the fort's granaries, just inside the west gate, produced evidence for a series of timber buildings. Coin evidence puts the final developments prior to these timber structures after AD 389, suggesting that the latter were built after ca 400. Building in timber was, in any case, not something normally done by the Roman army; and that alone would argue that the structures were erected after the military withdrawal – a conclusion given added weight by the fact that while one overlay the granary, the other was build over the road immediately outside the west gate and used the fort wall as a support; Roman military discipline would never have countenanced such a structure; so it was clearly no longer a factor with which the builders had to reckon.

These two buildings were followed by others. Little remains of the one just outside the fort wall but the one on the granary site was impressive, measuring twenty-three metres by eight metres and sixty centimetres. It may be seen as a grand hall, the central focus of the site in the fifth century. Similar buildings have been found dominating reoccupied iron-age hill-forts of the south west and Wales, at South Cadbury Castle, Cadbury Congresbury and Dinas

Powys for example. At Birdoswald we seem to have an initial phase of post-Roman occupation, followed by a grander building which may have lasted for some time. The ruler (or ruling body) based at the fort presumably took a while to consolidate his position and gather the resources necessary to undertake the larger construction.

The writings of St Patrick (see also p. 82 above) may add a little more depth to the study of archaeological developments at Birdoswald and other wall-forts in the fifth century. Patrick's precise date has its own problems, since his *Confession* and *Letters* give very few names or facts dateable from other sources. He says he was captured by Irish raiders at the age of sixteen and remained in Ireland for six years before escaping to Gaul. He returned to Ireland as bishop, sent as a missionary to the pagan Irish. Our late seventh-century *Life of St. Patrick* says that he was sent there by St. Germanus of Auxerre, who himself twice visited Britain to combat heresy; Germanus was consecrated as bishop of Auxerre *ca* AD 418, on the death of bishop Amator. So it is most unlikely that Patrick went back to Ireland before 418. In 431 Pope Celestine I appointed Palladius bishop of Ireland; and this is presented by the contemporary Prosper of Aquitane as a new development, his appointment marking the first attempt to bring Ireland within the ambit of the Catholic Church. Celestine was effectively creating an Irish diocese. Germanus, as bishop only of Auxerre, could hardly have done that on his own authority. He can only have been following Celestine's lead by appointing a second bishop either to support or to succeed Palladius. The second is more likely, since a second bishop would have required the creation of a second diocese, again something beyond Germanus' power.[46] As Germanus died *ca* 448, his appointment of Patrick must logically have occurred between 431 and 448. Later in that period would make more sense if we assume that Palladius spent any time in Ireland. To have reached a position in which he could be made a bishop, Patrick must have spent quite a time in Gaul with Germanus; he says in his *Confession* that he spent time in Gaul, then with his family in Britain, before returning again to Gaul to prepare himself for Ireland. The dating is rather vague but it is difficult to see Patrick as being born before about 410. His early life in Britain, therefore, must post-date the Roman withdrawal.

Just where in Britain Patrick came from has attracted much discussion. Somewhere in the west of Britain, in an area easily accessible by sea, has to be a given, since Patrick was captured by Irish raiders. His village, which he calls 'Bannavem Taberniae', is not otherwise known to us. Banna, however, was the Roman name for the fort at Birdoswald; an altar found there is dedicated to the deity Silvanus by the hunters of Banna. A village associated with the fort or even the fort itself, renamed to reflect its new function as the centre of a new power-structure, would be an obvious explanation for the name Bannavem Taberniae. Birdoswald is close to the Cumbrian coast; Irish raiders could land in the region of Carlisle in the absence of Roman troops and raid the surrounding area. The fort lies only fifteen or so miles from Carlisle. Name and location both fit; Patrick may well have come from Birdoswald.

The very existence of St Patrick and his writings tells us much about Hadrian's Wall during the fifth century, after the army and administration were withdrawn. His Christianity will be discussed below but here it is worth emphasising that he wrote in Latin. Not only could he read and write but he did so in classical Latin rather than the crude, debased Latin sometimes found on tombstones of the period. Vestiges of Roman education survived on into the fifth century, though this does not mean Patrick attended a school. Maybe his parents taught him Latin or employed a tutor. Whatever the truth of the matter, when Patrick sat down to write, he wrote in Latin. And that implies the existence of an audience who would understand him, that Latin, rather than a British dialect, remained in general use in Britain in the mid-fifth century. His use of Latin also demonstrates a certain frame of mind; it was a very Roman choice.

Patrick describes his father as a decurion. The curial class – the decurions – was traditionally the class from which the governors and magistrates of a city were drawn. Continued use of the rank need not imply that his father felt responsibility towards any city. It does, however, indicate an elite holding to a social position defined by the Roman system, even after the soldiers and administrators of that system had left. Society in what had been the frontier zone was still defining itself in Roman terms. Perhaps the grand, fifth-century, timber structure on the granary site at Birdoswald was the meeting place of a ruling council rather than the hall of a minor king.

From Patrick's description of his childhood we get the picture of a vibrant local community. It had priests and a social hierarchy – hence the mention of his father's social status. That status was not only secular but Christian. In providing background on himself and his childhood in the *Confession*, Patrick gives a sense of his position within the community; his father was a deacon, his grandfather a presbyter – both minor positions within the church hierarchy. Social position in the frontier zone during the fifth century was increasingly dependent upon the Church.

Christianity

In AD 313, Constantine, emperor of the western, and Licinius, emperor of the eastern Roman empire, jointly published the 'Edict of Milan', legalising Christianity for the first time. Constantine also gave huge support to the faith, presenting the Church with land, appointing Christians to posts in the imperial court, encouraging the religion within the army. This did not represent overnight success for Christianity but it certainly accelerated the process by which the religion came to dominate the empire. It had begun with the journeys of St. Paul and the other apostles, spreading the Christian message. Over the following two centuries or so, Christianity gained in influence, despite the overt disapproval of many emperors. More and more of the elite were converted, so that the Church grew richer and more powerful. The final stage in this process seems to have come in the late fourth century, when the emperor Theodosius outlawed pagan worship and closed down pagan temples.

However, despite the actions of both Constantine and Theodosius, evidence of a Christian presence in Britain before the sixth century remains weak. Only a few small churches of fourth- or fifth-century date are currently known, together with isolated examples of Christian art – such as the decorated wall-plaster from Lullingstone villa or the mosaic depicting Christ from the villa at Hinton St Mary – and a number of later stories about British saints, such as St Alban. Alban was associated by Gildas in the sixth century with the Roman city of Verulamium (St Albans). The Christian theologian and heretic Pelagius, whose writings survive, was British, though he did not live or write in Britain.

Evidence for Christian activity on Hadrian's Wall matches this rather vague picture. Historians have tried to suggest that Carlisle was a Christian centre but the evidence is not good. Cities were, on the whole, the seats of bishops and at least three bishops are attested in the island during the fourth century; they are recorded as having attended major Church councils at Arles in AD 314, Nicaea (modern Iznik in Turkey) in 325, Serdica (modern Sofia in Bulgaria) in 343 and Ariminium (Rimini in Italy) in 359/60. In none of these cases are the cities from which the bishops came recorded. It has been suggested that the four British bishops at the Council of Arles represented the cities which governed the four provinces into which Diocletian had divided Britain.[47] The Gallic bishops who attended were certainly from provincial capitals. If – and it is, as the discussion above shows, a big 'if' – Carlisle was a provincial capital, then its bishop may have gone to Arles. That conclusion, however, involves building supposition upon supposition. The only hard evidence of Christianity at Carlisle is a single tombstone; to move from that to a bishopric and a northern Christian centre would be unwise.

The tombstone, nonetheless, suggests the presence of Christians in Carlisle. It dates to the fourth century and records a man named Flavius Antigonus Papias, whose name may indicate that he came from the Greek east; Christianity, deriving from the eastern part of the empire in the first place, was far more widespread there than in the west during the third and fourth centuries. Flavius is not specifically described as a Christian but the tombstone uses the phrase *animam revocavit* (he recalled his soul) – a very Christian way of looking at death. Pagan Roman religions had concepts of an afterlife but the notion of souls being sent and recalled was a Christian one.

There is other evidence for a Christian presence in the frontier zone in late antiquity. At Maryport, on the Cumbrian coast, a (now lost) *chi-rho* symbol – a P (*rho*) with an X (*chi*) above to give the first two letters (ch and r) of Christ's name in Greek – was found. It is possible, too, that church buildings exist at Vindolanda, Housesteads and Birdoswald. Identification of early churches is usually difficult, because they vary in shape and size. The buildings found at these three forts were very much to a standard plan, all aligned east-west, as expected in a church (mediaeval and modern churches and graves always face east, the direction from which Christ will come at the end of the world), with an apse on the western end. The design matches that of a late Roman church at Silchester – perhaps our best example of a British, Christian church from the period. We can be reasonably confident that all three buildings at the forts were churches. Their precise dating, in the absence of much coinage, is difficult; but all three seem to have been built around the end of the fourth century, constructed either by the army or, after its departure, by those who continued to use these sites. They continued in use for some time; so, whether or not the army was responsible for their original construction, the three forts continued to function as Christian centres after the military withdrawal.

Again St Patrick adds to the archaeological evidence. Identification of Birdoswald (Banna) as his home reinforces the fifth century Christian presence in the area of the wall. In his *Confession* he implies a strong Christian community; they were all (himself included), he says, bad Christians who did not listen to their priests; their capture by Irish raiders was God's punishment on them. God's punishment is a familiar Christian trope of this period; Gildas had also used it – and so did many Gallic writers. The message is clear: Patrick's audience should repent their sins and turn fully to God, if they not to be harshly punished. A modicum of truth lies behind the sermonising. He *was* captured and taken to Ireland; and we can argue that he *was* part of a thriving Christian community. For he is not creating a fictional experience; rather he is interpreting what actually happened to him and attributing it to the will of God. In his account we can see the vibrancy of the frontier's Christian community.

It is on this basis that we may infer a Christian centre at Carlisle. In most areas it holds true that Christianity was disseminated from one place; for in late antiquity particular bishops and priests were the major local source of Christian teaching. They were based almost exclusively in cities; indeed from late antique Gaul we get a distinct impression that the city had been adopted by the Church as a Christian entity, that the city's bishop took responsibility for Christian care and conversion of the surrounding area. The problem with applying this model to Hadrian's Wall is that in the militarised area there was another source of Christian faith.

Constantine and his successors had put considerable effort into converting the army, which would have had more contact in and around the forts with ordinary people than a church hierarchy in Carlisle could ever have. Evidence for Christainity in the region does not necessarily mean the presence of a bishop.

The existence of churches in the forts during the fifth century is an interesting development. They may well post-date the withdrawal of the army and they were certainly in use at the time when the forts were becoming the centres for local fiefdoms. In Gaul the Church was becoming associated with local power structures; the bishops, drawn from the local elites, were effectively governing the cities. The discovery of churches on the wall in the sub-Roman power centres suggests a similar development. Christianity had become crucial to daily life; its churches occupied a position within local administrative centres and Christian status, as St Patrick demonstrates, was a crucial component of social position. With the removal of the army and the development of Christianity, the structure of society on Hadrian's Wall was changing.

The Christian presence is also interesting for what it tells us about Britain's place within the western empire. It shows that she was still clearly thought of as a part of the western, catholic, Church, increasingly centred upon the Pope and on Rome. The *Life of St Germanus of Auxerre*, written at the end of the fifth century by Constantius of Lyon, purports to record the visit of Germanus to Britain to stamp out the false teachings of the heretic Pelagius. Hagiography, of course, is not biography and should not be taken as fact; its aim was to present Christian ideals for the education of the reader. The story of Germanus' visit is, however, useful as evidence, not because it is true but because Constantius regarded it as reasonable that Germanus might visit Britain. This in itself demonstrates that the Church in Gaul felt Britain still fell within its sphere of influence and responsibility even as late as the end of the fifth century, that it (including Hadrian's Wall) was part of an organisation which not only spanned the western empire but was, as bishops grew in power and emperors paraded their Christianity, becomingly increasingly synonymous with Roman government and administration. So, even after the army and the administrators had gone, leaving a power vacuum on the northern frontier, the Christian presence there meant that the region was still, in some sense, under Roman influence. Hadrian's Wall had begun life by marking the power and imperial credentials of the emperor Hadrian; in the fifth century the wall was still a part of the Roman empire, albeit in very different, church terms.

Chapter 6

Conclusion: Hadrian's Wall
and the English sense of history

A twenty-first-century historian's view is inevitably the product, on the one hand, of centuries of past scholarship and, on the other, of his or her own contemporary experience. In the case of Hadrian's Wall our current ideas and comments may come to seem as dated as the eighteenth-century belief – that it should be attributed to Severus – now seems to us. Scholarship always reflects the academic traditions of its own time; and our judgements about the wall are filtered through an accretion of knowledge collected since at least the eighteenth century. We cannot each carry out our own excavations as and when we require fresh information; we have to rely on those of others and on the way in which they have been presented to us – something shaped by the academic traditions of the time when they were carried out. On Hadrian's Wall, decisions about where to excavate – which areas of a site are regarded as most significant – were taken on the basis of current academic trends. For the past two or three hundred years, in particular, those trends have been set by a strong sense of British – or, more accurately, English – history. Far from being free of ideological bias, archaeology and history are particularly susceptible to it, because ideas of nationhood are highly dependent on a sense of the past. In a vicious circle, what the historian or archaeologist is taught in his or her early years affects, consciously or unconsciously, their picture of the past. Their scholarship is then presented as fact to the next generation; so the circle continues. Even when academic assumptions are challenged, popular culture is much slower to adjust.

Our current view of Hadrian's Wall is as much an ideological construct as a physical one. A theme of this book has been the frustration that, while much is known about the Roman army on the wall, we understand far less about the native population. We can discuss the forts of the wall in detail but not the *vici* or the city of Carlisle; that we know more about Corbridge than about Carlisle stems from the fact that the town lies largely over the earlier, military fort. The problem has its roots in the English sense of history.

Early study of Hadrian's Wall

The earliest studies of Hadrian's Wall predate the development of archaeology as a means of investigating the past. Antiquarians of the sixteenth, seventeenth and eighteenth centuries treated only those remains which could be seen above ground. Inevitably, then, these men concentrated on the forts and the wall itself – and so on the Roman army. Those were the most visible remains of the Roman presence. This is not to say that they were without an ideological bias. Camden, for instance, presented the Roman army as a Christian institution, helping to create a British Church; writing in the aftermath of the Reformation, he was concerned to justify the existence of an Anglican Church independent of the Papacy and used his picture of an early British Church as an historical precedent. Horsley wanted to show that the Roman remains of Britain were as interesting as those of the continent. General Roy, who mapped the area north of Hadrian's Wall and Roman Scotland in the aftermath of the 1745 Jacobite rebellion, was driven in his work by feelings of affinity with a Roman army, which he saw as a model of efficiency and rational organisation. This is understandable, given that he owed his position in the army to ability rather than birth – a circumstance which put him in a minority.[48] None of the antiquarians, however, has as much effect upon our view of Hadrian's Wall as did the nineteenth- and early twentieth-century excavators, whose ideologies have thus left us such a one-sided view of the wall.

The teaching of history

The teaching of history and of classics, especially during the nineteenth century, has done much to shape academic study of the Roman world in general and of Hadrian's Wall in particular. The study of Greek and Roman writers with an interest in history was central to education in these subjects. Our sense of what 'history' is, of those aspects which deserve attention and study, has thus been shaped by the preoccupations of the historians of the ancient world. This is partly because it is easier to write history dictated by the interests of our primary sources. In the ancient world historians recorded events – battles, the reigns of emperors, political developments – with a sideline in biographies of great men, presented didactically as moral ideals to which others might aspire. Thus, the easiest kind of history to write from the work of, say, Thucydides, Tacitus or Suetonius is their kind of history. We can compare and contrast accounts to produce assessments of the actions and characters of emperors, statesmen and armies.

More subtly, it was ancient writers who first formed a sense of what history should be. It was Thucydides, in the *History of the Peloponnesian War* written towards the end of the fifth century BC, who formulated the idea that the historian should be as objective as possible, that he should test his sources and not simply write down the first story that came his way. Thucydides was succeeded by centuries of Greek and Roman historians, the best of whom – those most often studied in later periods – followed Thucydidean methods to a lesser or greater degree. Their sense of historical method, of historical topic and theme, was picked up in the eighteenth and nineteenth centuries by scholars trained in Latin and Greek, products of an educational system which placed training in the classical languages at the centre of school life; they were thus used to reading the work of the Greek and Roman historians.[49] Budding historians of recent centuries read Thucydides and Tacitus as children, adopting their approach to history. Historical agendas in the eighteenth and nineteenth centuries – and even now – were set in the ancient world. So a great deal of historical writing concentrates upon military and political matters. Socio-economic and cultural history are quite recently developed branches of historical studies in general and ancient studies in particular. Even now, the programmes of academic conferences are often dominated by papers concentrating on political and biographical matters.

The nineteenth-century clergymen, gentlemen and squires who undertook the first excavations on Hadrian's Wall had been educated to search for evidence of soldiers and administrators.

Such men, after all, were the stuff of proper historical investigation. The belief that military matters were crucial to accounts of the past is reflected in Edward Gibbon's seminal work of the late eighteenth century, *The Decline and Fall of the Roman Empire*. The key to both Roman success and failure, Gibbon argued, lay with the Roman army. In earlier periods its bravery and discipline had created the empire; later it became corrupt, incompetent and ill-disciplined, so that it was unable to repel the barbarian hordes which Gibbon saw as the major factor in the demise of Roman civilisation. That Gibbon saw the army as so significant – indeed, that he saw the end of empire in terms of military defeat rather than the cultural evolution envisioned by so many modern scholars – reflects those factors which the eighteenth and nineteenth centuries saw as significant to the study of the ancient world. Excavations thus focussed on forts to the exclusion of almost everything else. The way in which history was taught and pursued, however, was far from being the only reason for the concentration of nineteenth- and early twentieth-century researchers on the military aspects of Hadrian's Wall.

The Romans and the English

In the course of the nineteenth century, the idea that there were some links between the English and the Romans became increasingly popular.[50] For much of the eighteenth century and some of the nineteenth the English had not looked towards Rome at all. It was the classical Greeks, with their love of freedom, who were considered more worthy of study, while historical accounts of the destruction of Roman Britain by the Anglo-Saxons suggested that the racial origins of the English lay with the latter. Romans were seen as decadent and tyrannical, while the freedom of the Greeks and the pastoral existence of the Saxons were much closer to the idealised nineteenth-century English way of life. As the British empire expanded, however, the Roman empire came increasingly to be seen as its forerunner. Interest in Roman history grew and with it the belief that in some way there was a connection between the English and the Romans, that the Romans had played a key part in 'creating' the English.

Archaeological excavation played a key role in this, especially on Hadrian's Wall. Roman monuments were a tangible link between Rome and modern Britain; their concrete presence gave Rome a key place in the development of English history. The sheer size of the wall made it a massively obvious testament to England's past and from the eighteenth century it attracted sightseers. Indeed its existence has lead to parts of the history of Newcastle and Gateshead being presented in Roman terms. A striking example is the Gateshead memorial to the fallen of the First World War (figs. 24 and 25). Their valour is commemorated by depiction of a Roman soldier; military endeavour is seen in Roman terms, which thus constitute a key part of Gateshead's community history.

The view that the Romans played a key role in creating the English is found most simply in the children's history book *Our Island Story*, written by H.E. Marshall (first published 1905). Children's history books are particularly indicative; for they make little attempt to disguise their ideological agenda. English history is presented by Marshall as a series of developments which give rise to a heavily idealised modern England. The initial chapters show heroic ancient Britons holding out against the tyrannical Romans; the invading Romans are seen in very negative terms. Then, in a complete *volte face*, they become benevolent rulers, bringing civilisation. Against their wise government the British rebel, forcing them to leave Britain. The Saxons then arrive, first as blood-thirsty invaders, then as another important and beneficial development in Britain's history. Marshall's narrative creates a series of problems and inconsistencies which are never dealt with; the ideology which claims the English will never allow themselves to be conquered conflicts with the late nineteenth-century insistence that the Romans were an important part of English history. It is a paradox that Marshall never resolves.

In some senses, she picked up and tried to combine all strands of nineteenth-century thinking about the origins of the English, in an attempt to create a cohesive sense of English nationalism. Brief separation of these strands is worthwhile; for each had its impact upon historical and archaeological investigation – and on the study of Hadrian's Wall. Marshall was clearly influenced by what Hingley has termed the 'Teutonic origin myth' of the English – the belief that, such was the devastating impact of the Saxon invasions, Roman civilisation was swept away; the Saxons

Fig. 24 The War Memorial in Gateshead

Fig. 25 Detail of the War Memorial in Gateshead

should, therefore, be seen as genetic ancestors of the English.[51] Those who subscribed to this belief but nonetheless wished to link the Romans and the English, were forced to argue the former provided a cultural inheritance. G. Norwood, Headmaster of Bristol Grammar School, for instance, argued that teaching classics to schoolboys provided an invaluable service to the entire country, since study of the Roman empire could teach the English much about governing their own.

This was a line of thinking which remained popular into the twentieth century. In this context the ideas of Stanley Baldwin (British Prime Minister in 1923 and again in 1924-9 and 1935-7) are interesting. As a man with a strong background in the classics – he was cousin of Rudyard Kipling, nephew of the pre-Raphaelite painter E.J. Poynter and a president of the Classical Association – he had a good awareness of Britain's Roman past. In a speech (in 1926) to the Classical Association, for example, he argued that the modern English nation had been forged on the anvil of ancient Rome. The image of construction employed by Baldwin is inescapable, so that the audience would have been left in no doubt that Rome played a key role in creating the English. Indeed the use of the anvil seems especially significant: Rome becomes the tool which produces the finished product; the two empires are thus not only linked but the English are placed in a superior position to the Romans.

It was important for nineteenth- and twentieth-century thinkers that this should be the case. Since Gibbon's *Decline and Fall*, the popular model of Rome's end was one of collapse and disaster; if Rome was felt to provide a cultural inheritance for the English and if the Roman empire was forerunner of the British empire, then it was important for the English that they avoid Rome's fate. Benjamin Disraeli, who as Prime Minister made Victoria Empress of India, was particularly preoccupied with this topic. In much of his writing he muses on the ruins and the fate of Rome. In the superiority of the English, as Baldwin later believed, lay their hope of escape from this doom. They could learn from Rome's mistakes as well as from her successes.

Nineteenth-century thinkers who followed this line believed that the two Empires had much in common: both were ruled by a sovereign; both relied upon courage in the face of adversity; both were pragmatic and turned fine intellects to practical problems such as engineering; both had an innate capacity for ruling.[52] Both empires were to be applauded for bringing civilisation to the uncivilised. Notions of Roman tyranny were, perforce, quickly dropped when Victoria became empress of India in 1876; the Roman empire as a model for the British had become so popular that to accuse Romans of despotism would be to impute the same to the English.

Parallels between the Romans in Britain and the British in India became inescapable; indeed, as Norwood suggested, the parallel between the two was useful, since Rome provided a model of ideal governance for future administrators of India. At the same time as educators and administrators drew on the Roman government of Britain as a model, British rule in India became a model on which academics drew in their study of the Romans in Britain. Their accounts of operations on the Roman frontiers were founded on the British experience in India (see also p. 21 above). The Romans were seen as occupying Britain in the same way as the British lived in India – a separate population ruling subservient natives. Villas, towns and forts were the homes of administrators and soldiers who lived quite apart from a primitive native population in their timber round-houses. As the fledgling discipline of Roman-British archaeology developed, it was the villas, towns and forts that formed its raw material; native settlements were primitive, non-Roman and not worth study. Attention paid to them – on the model of British India – implicitly gave status to the Indians as a subject deserving of study.

Alongside this view of the Romans in Britain there developed the idea that they had provided a genetic inheritance for the English. Some scholars and writers believed that, far from living separately from the British population, they intermarried to create a 'Romano-British' population. Similarly, when the Saxons came to Britain, they did not kill off the Romano-British but bred with them to produce a synthesis – the best of the Romans *and* the Saxons.

Intermarriage between Romans and Britons is a notion found particularly in the works of Rudyard Kipling. His poem *The Roman Centurion's Song* is the lament of an officer ordered back to Rome after forty years in Britain, who now feels more affinity with

Britain than with Italy. At the level of children's literature, *Puck of Pook's Hill* (first published in 1906) – a more subtle account of what it meant to be English than that provided by Marshall – includes the story of a centurion serving on the wall at the end of the fourth century AD. His name is Parnesius, born on the Isle of White and serving the usurper Maximus. Throughout Parnesius is at once a Roman soldier but clearly a Briton. Maximus' rebellion is presented as a heroic British enterprise: Britain stands alone against the rest of the world.

English greatness is seen here as the result of a mixing of races. Indeed *Puck of Pook's Hill* continually sees English history as a series of invasions, each invader ultimately settling in England and adding vital qualities to her character. This should, theoretically, have given much more status to study of the native population. In fact it did no such thing; there was still no room for the Celts. Kipling begins his history in *Puck* with the Romans firmly part of the British population; there is no consideration of pre-Roman native peoples. For scholars who followed this line Romans were a necessary part of the English character. Without them, development of the Britons into the English would have been impossible; so only those who became Romanised, living like Romans in towns and villas, deserved study.

The same remained true of archaeology on Hadrian's Wall. Nineteenth- and early twentieth-century excavators were interested only in villas, towns and forts. On Hadrian's Wall, there were no villas and only two towns – one of them inaccessible beneath modern Carlisle. So archaeologists studied only forts and the wall itself. From the very first excavations concentrated on military matters; the civilian population was forgotten. Political ideologies current in the nineteenth century dictated the archaeological, as much as the historical, agenda; and in the early twentieth the same continued to be true. Haverfield (see pp. 84-5 above), the first professional Romano-British archaeologist, was hugely influential in the development of the discipline. He believed the Anglo-Saxon invasions had swept Roman civilisation from Britain, so that its values had to be reintroduced from the continent during the Renaissance. At the same time he believed (as did Kipling) that Romans and Britons had become a single population, their lives revolving around towns and villas. The problem with this view was that in Wales and the north of England the native population had not become Romanised; excavations by Haverfield's nineteenth-century predecessors had concentrated on forts, where there was no evidence of a Romanised population. He therefore developed a model still, often subconsciously, current today: that of a civilian zone in southern Britain, where the population became fully Romanised; and a military zone in the west and north, where the army provided the only vestige of civilisation. Haverfield's view was dictated by nineteenth-century political agendas; but it has all too often continued to set the terms of debate in the modern study of Hadrian's Wall. Frequently the wall is interpreted only in military terms. Aspects of civilian life are under-explored, their significance frequently down-played or ignored. The bias has its roots deep in nineteenth-century ideas of the proper material for historical study and of the Roman role in English history and in the development of the English character.

In practical terms this means that the wall, as now presented to visitors, is difficult to view and understand in terms other than those defined by Haverfield and his predecessors. It is true that maps and museums the length of the wall include the civilian settlements; reconstructions of the site in miniature at both Birdoswald and Chesters, for example, incorporate buildings intended to represent the *vici*. At Housesteads the map in the car park – the first piece of information available to any visitor – includes the fort's *vicus*. However, anyone hoping to make an easy identification of the settlements' strip-houses (see pp. 66-7 above) may well be disappointed. At all three sites key military buildings inside the fort's walls are exposed, sign-posted and explained; nothing of the *vicus* is to be seen at Chesters, while at Housesteads and Birdoswald the visitor must carefully memorise the map and reconstuction in order to associate a collection of bumps in the ground with the *vicus*. The presence of the civilian settlement has at least been registered and that is a step forward but it is no more than a small advance.

The exception is Vindolanda. Years of excavation there by the Birley family have resulted in a shift of attention from the fort itself to the surrounding area; the *vicus* has been painstakingly uncovered. Strip houses and even a temple are open to visitors, enabling them to gain a fuller picture of life as a whole – civilian as well as military – at Vindolanda. The site also provides several full-scale reconstructions of strip houses and shops, while wax models also bring the visitor face to face with the merchants who inhabited the area. That Vindolanda offers this merely emphasises the short-comings at other sites. Even so Vindolanda itself is far from perfect in this respect; for nineteenth-century assumptions – that military considerations are more significant than civilian – linger on. Within the *vicus* – but close to the fort wall – additional barracks were erected in the early third century; and it is these that are laid out and signed for the visitor rather than the strip houses which they supplanted. Even at Vindolanda the military remains are privileged at the expense of the civilian.

Conclusions

To study Hadrian's Wall at the beginning of the twenty-first century is to draw on a wealth of material that throws light on its military aspects. We know where the soldiers came from, what they wore, how they fought, how they spent their free time, what they ate and where their supplies came from. We know about their forts and a great deal about the wall's construction. Yet this vast body of knowledge tends to distort our approach to other aspects of the subject. We have military matters uppermost in our minds, so that we are pre-conditioned to see in the wall a series of defensive barriers, not an ideological frontier within an entire frontier zone. We see continued use of the wall-forts in the fifth century not as centres for civilian administration but as maintaining a military aspect. This book has attempted to redress that balance. And, unless agendas change and move away from nineteenth-century modes of thinking, unless archaeological excavations begin to pay more attention to civilian matters, it will remain very difficult to draw firm conclusions about civilian life on the wall. More *vici* and native farmsteads must be excavated, to complete our picture of life in the frontier zone. If we maintain Haverfield's original notion that all of northern England was simply an uncivilised, un-Romanised military zone, quite different from the Romanised south, then we will continue to fail on two counts: we will not look beyond the military aspects of the wall; and we will continue to ask the wrong questions of our evidence.

Notes

Chapter 1
1. For a more detailed consideration of the motivations of Caesar and Claudius in invading Britain and details of their campaigns, see P. Salway, *A History of Roman Britain* (Oxford University Press, 1997) chs 1-3.
2. It has been suggested that Trajan was himself responsible for the construction of a frontier system along the Tyne-Solway isthmus. For discussion of the question, see D. Breeze and B. Dobson, *Hadrian's Wall* (Penguin, London, 2000), 13-24.
3. Breeze and Dobson (note 2 above) 30.
4. For further discussion of the construction of the *vallum*, see Breeze and Dobson (note 2 above) 56-9.
5. For further discussion of Diocletian's provincial reorganisation (which has little impact upon the above discussion), see Salway (note 1 above) 289-93.
6. Figures drawn from M. Hassall, 'The Army', in A.K. Bowman, P.Garnsey and D. Rathbone (eds), *The High Empire: AD 70-192* (= vol. 11, *Cambridge Ancient History*, 2nd edn, 2000) 322-4. For the organisation of the army in Britain, see also ch. 3 below.
7. This summarises the chapter 'The background to Romanisation' in R. Reece, *My Roman Britain* (Cotswold Studies, Cirencester, 1988).
8. For Hadrian's Wall as part of a more modern landscape, see J. Crow and R.Woodside, *Hadrian's Wall: An Historic Landscape* (National Trust, London, 1999). (The reconstruction of an eighteenth-century crofter's cottage at Vindolanda is of interest in this connection.)
9. The relationship between archaeological and textual evidence is frequently misunderstood: many historians of the ancient world regard archaeology simply as a way of 'filling in the gaps' in information provided by the literary record; archaeologists, on the other hand, tend to point, with some justification, to areas in which archaeology has proved texts wrong. The problem is that each form

of evidence answers different kinds of question about the ancient world, though some ancient historians and archaeologists do not always seem to appreciate that. See J. Moreland, *Archaeology and Text* (Duckworth, London, 2001) and N. Morley, *Writing Ancient History* (Duckworth, London, 1999).

Chapter 2

10. Virgil, *Aeneid* 1.278-9.

11. C.R. Whittaker, *Frontiers of the Roman Empire: A Social and Economic Study* (John Hopkins University Press, Baltimore and London, 1994); also 'Frontiers' in Bowman, Garnsey and Rathbone (note 6 above) 293-319.

12. C. Wells, '*Profuit invitis te dominante capi*: Social and Economic Considerations on the Roman Frontiers' in *Journal of Roman Archaeology* 9 (1996) 436-46.

13. Whittaker, 'Frontiers' (note 11 above) 294.

14. Wells (note 12 above) 438.

15. Breeze and Dobson (note 2 above) 16.

16. On the significance of city walls, see further Whittaker, 'Frontiers' (note 11 above) 294-5; and J. Rykwert, *The Idea of a Town. The Anthropology of Urban Form in Rome, Italy and the Ancient World* (MIT Press, London, 1988).

17. Breeze and Dobson (note 2 above) 56-9.

18. I.A. Richmond, 'Britannia Inferior' in P. Salway (ed.), *Roman Archaeology and Art: Essays and Studies by Sir Ian Richmond* (Faber and Faber, London, 1969) 62.

19. Whittaker, 'Frontiers' (note 11 above) 295.

Chapter 3

20. Breeze and Dobson (note 2 above) 54.

21. For the detail of which units built which parts of the wall, see Breeze and Dobson (note 2 above) ch. 2.

22. Breeze and Dobson (note 2 above) 157.

23. Hassall (note 6 above) 320-2.

24. Hassall (note 6 above) 332.

25. Breeze and Dobson (note 2 above) 53.

26. Breeze and Dobson (note 2 above) 159-60.

27. The *Saturnalia* was the Roman New Year celebration – an excuse for feasting and parties.

28. J. Bennett and E. Scott, 'The End of Roman Settlement in Northern England (with an Appendix on Romano-British Wheat Yields)' in J.C. Chapman and H.C. Mytum (eds), *Settlement in North Britain 1000BC – AD1000* (Oxford, 1983) 206 ff. Their figures are based on work done at Butser Farm in Hampshire, which is run, so far as possible, using Iron Age farming techniques. Conditions cannot be precisely replicated but the work done there is valuable since it gives historians and archaeologists some possible figures for food yields.
29. Ammianus Marcellinus, 18.2.3-6.
30. Tacitus, *Agricola*, 19.
31. Whittaker, *Frontiers of the Roman Empire* (note 11 above) 105-6.
32. P. Bidwell, *Roman Forts in Britain* (Batsford, London, 1997) 87.
33. Chesters and Vindolanda both provide good examples of excavated fort bath-houses, while Wallsend has a full reconstruction based on evidence from across the Roman empire.
34. For an imaginative – but still interesting – account of Mithraism in action, see Mary Stewart's Arthurian novel, *The Crystal Cave*.

Chapter 4

35. Bidwell (note 32 above) 72-3.
36. Bidwell (note 32 above) 75-6.
37. Bidwell (note 32 above) 73.
38. Bidwell (note 32 above) 76-7
39. Hingley, *Roman Officers and English Gentlemen* (Routledge, London, 2000) chs 9 and 10.

Chapter 5

40. Broadly speaking, most scholars would, I believe, incline to the view that the end of the Roman empire cannot be tied down to a single date, not least because the process by which the Roman Empire became mediaeval Europe varied from area to area. Rome recovered from the Gothic attack; a Roman emperor continued to exist in the eastern part of the Roman Empire after 476; and the Germanic kings of Gaul paid homage to him and, indeed, owed their position to their integration into the Roman elite classes. The end of Rome could even be assigned to the fall of the Austro-Hungarian Holy Roman Empire in 1914; or it is possible to see the Pope in the Vatican as presiding over a modern Roman Empire, defined by adherence to catholicism. It depends on one's standpoint.

41. Ideally, everything on a site – every level, every piece of evidence – should be recorded. Even now, however, levels above those in which an excavator is interested are all too often thrown away. (I worked on a site in Gloucestershire where everything post-mediaeval was discarded as rubbish, though it gave an interesting view of the village's post-mediaeval existence).

42. For a readable guide to coinage, see Reece (note 7 above).

43. See, for example, the *Book of Amos*.

44. For more detail, see S. Esmonde Cleary, *The Ending of Roman Britain* (Routledge, London, 1989) 136-9.

45. Bidwell (note 32 above) 108.

46. If Germanus was responsible for appointing an Irish bishop, he was effectively bringing the Irish diocese within the sway of the diocese of Auxerre. Patrick would always owe his position to Germanus.

47. J. Wacher, *The Towns of Roman Britain* (Batsford, London, 1995) 84.

Chapter 6

48. For more details, see Bidwell (note 32 above) 19.

49. It may be worth noting, just as an example, that of the seven original Chairs – professorial posts – instituted by Henry Overton Wills in the nineteenth century when he founded the University of Bristol, two were in Classics, one each in Latin and in Greek. This reflects the privileged position of Classics as a subject at this time.

50. It should be emphasised that the link was explicitly made between Romans and English (not between Romans and *British*). English writers drew distinct lines between English culture and that of the Welsh and Scots, terming them 'Celtic' and using classical accounts of their barbarism to justify the distinction. The English insisted that they – not the Welsh and Scots – were the true descendants of the Romans.

51. Hingley (note 39 above) 145.

52. R.F. Betts, 'The Allusions to Rome in British Imperialist Thought of the Late Nineteenth and Early Twentieth Centuries' in *Victorian Studies* 15.2 (Dec. 1971) 152.

Further reading

Chapter 1

A more traditional, chronological history of Roman Britain is provided by P. Salway, *A History of Roman Britain* (Oxford University Press, 1997). M. Millett, *The Romanization of Britain* (Cambridge University Press, 1990) gives an excellent account of the socio-economic development of Britain under Roman rule, while R. Reece, *My Roman Britain* (Cotswold Studies, Cirencester, 1988) provides a useful guide to both socio-economic matters and the problems of using archaeological evidence. For a guide to the wall, the best start is R.J.A. Wilson, *A Guide to the Roman Remains in Britain* (Constable, London, 1988) ch. 8. Books specifically concerned with Hadrian's Wall are numerous: D.J. Breeze and B. Dobson, *Hadrian's Wall* (Penguin, London, 2000) is probably the best – enormously detailed and thorough. There is also S. Johnson, *Hadrian's Wall* (Batsford, London, 1989). The history of study of the wall is treated by P. Bidwell, *Roman Forts in Britain* (Batsford, London, 1997) ch. 1; and by S. Johnson, *Rome and its Empire* (Routledge, London, 1989) ch. 1. Younger readers – and older ones too – may enjoy Rosemary Sutcliffe's three books set on Hadrian's Wall: *The Eagle of the Ninth* (most recently Oxford University Press, 2003), *The Silver Branch* (most recently Oxford University Press, 2001) and *Frontier Wolf* (most recently Puffin Books, 1984).

Chapter 2

The best work on frontiers in general has been done by C.R. Whittaker, *Frontiers of the Roman Empire: A Social and Economic Study* (John Hopkins University Press, Baltimore and London, 1994); also his article 'Frontiers' in A.K. Bowman, P. Garnsey and D. Rathbone (eds), *The High Empire: AD 70-192* (= vol 11, *Cambridge Ancient History*, 2nd edn, 2000). C.M. Wells has provided an overview of work on the subject in his article '*Profuit invitis te dominante capi*: Social and Economic Considerations on the Roman Frontiers' in *Journal of Roman Archaeology* 9 (1996) 436-46.

Specifically on Hadrian's Wall as a frontier, it is well worth reading D. Breeze and B. Dobson, *Hadrian's Wall* chs.1 and 2; on the *vallum*, see their pp. 56-9, along with I.A. Richmond, 'Britannia Inferior' in P. Salway (ed.), *Roman Archaeology and Art: Essays and Studies by Sir Ian Richmond* (Faber and Faber, London, 1969). For more detail on Hadrian, A.R. Birley, *Hadrian: the Restless Emperor* (Routledge, London, 1997) is worthwhile.

Chapter 3

A well-written, very readable starting point for study of the Roman army in Britain is P. Bidwell, *Roman Forts in Britain* (1997). Breeze and Dobson (see ch. 2 above) are very much concerned with military matters throughout, though in this context their chs. 5 and 6 are particularly useful. Books on the topic are legion but G. Webster, *The Roman Imperial Army* (Black, London, 1985) is among the best. M. Hassall, 'The Army' in vol. 11, *Cambridge Ancient History* is also useful. Figures for supply of the army come from J. Bennett and E. Scott, 'The end of Roman Settlement in Northern England (with an appendix on Romano-British Wheat Yields)' in J.C. Chapman and H.C. Mytum (eds), *Settlement in North Britain 1000 BC – AD 1000* (British Archaeological Reports, Oxford, 1983). Also of use is D. Breeze, 'Demand and Supply on the Northern Frontier' in P. Clack and S. Haselgrove (eds), *Rural Settlement in the Roman North* (Durham University Press, 1982). The best book on the Vindolanda tablets is A.K. Bowman, *Life and Letters on the Roman Frontier: Vindolanda and its People* (British Museum, London, 1994); this useful analysis also includes a selection of tablets translated into English.

Chapter 4

Civilian settlements (*vici*) have attracted less attention than they deserve; Bidwell (see under ch. 3 above) provides a good guide to the topic. The best book on the cities of Britain is J. Wacher, *The

Towns of Roman Britain (Batsford, London, 1995); P. Ottaway, *Archaeology in British Towns: from the Emperor Claudius to the Black Death* (Routledge, London,1992) is also interesting. Richmond, 'Britannia Inferior' (see under ch. 2 above) gives an overview of Corbridge and Carlisle: little has been published on Corbridge but Carlisle has been covered in more detail in M. McCarthy, *Roman Carlisle and the Lands of the Solway* (Tempus, Stroud, 2002). No detailed account of rural life in the northern frontier zone exists, though R. Hingley has provided a useful survey of the evidence and the issues in 'Rural Settlement in Northern Britain' in M. Todd (ed.), *A Companion to Roman Britain* (Blackwell, Oxford, 2003). Also helpful is G. Jobey, 'Homesteads and Settlements of the Frontier Area' in C. Thomas (ed.), *Rural Settlement in Roman Britain* (Council for British Archaeology, London, 1966). McCarthy, *Roman Carlisle* (see above), chs 6 and 7, is also helpful. Issues of terminology in discussing Romanisation have been raised by R. Hingley, *Roman Officers and English Gentlemen* (Routledge, London, 2000) chs 9 and 10.

Chapter 5

The most comprehensive book on the end of Roman Britain is A. S. Esmonde Cleary, *The Ending of Roman Britain* (Routledge, London, 1989). M.E. Jones, *The End of Roman Britain* (Cornell University Press, Ithaca and London, 1996) also has points of interest, not least its critical response to the very dated notion that Saxon invaders were responsible for the end of Roman Britain. Readers looking for a more general account of the period may turn to A. Cameron, *The Later Roman Empire* (Fontana, London, 1993); then to P. Brown, *The World of late Antiquity* (Thames & Hudson, London, 1971). The history of Birdoswald has been usefully presented for the general reader by T. Wilmott, *Birdoswald* (Tempus, Stroud, 2000); and more detailed examination of its end can be found in the same author's 'Collapse Theory and the End of Birdoswald' in P. Rush (ed.), *Theoretical Roman Archaeology: Second Conference Proceedings* (Ashgate Publishing, Aldershot, 1995). On late Roman settlement changes, the relevant chapters of Breeze and Dobson (see under ch. 1 above) and Bidwell (see under ch. 3 above) are useful though brief; that no detailed

124 HADRIAN'S WALL AND ITS PEOPLE

survey exists reflects the state of scholarship on the subject. Two useful books on the development of Christianity are P. Brown, *The Rise of Western Christendom* (Blackwell, Oxford, 1996) and H. Chadwick, *The Early Church* (Penguin, London, 1993). On the tricky subject of Christianity in Britain, see C. Thomas, *Christianity in Roman Britain to AD 500* (Batsford, London, 1981).

Chapter 6

Much work has been done in recent years on the uses made of Rome by the Victorians. R. Hingley, *Roman Officers and English Gentlemen* (Routledge, London, 2000) provides an extremely useful survey of the topic. The same author has also edited a collection of articles, *Images of Rome. Perceptions of Ancient Rome in Europe and the United States in the Modern Age* (= *Journal of Roman Archaeology*, Supplementary Series no.44, 2001); his articles in the volume, 'Images of Rome' and 'An Imperial Legacy: the Contribution of Classical Rome to the Character of the English' are well worth reading. Also useful is R. F. Betts, 'The Allusion to Rome in British Imperialist Thought of the Late Nineteenth and Early Twentieth Centuries' in *Victorian Studies* 15.2 (Dec. 1971) 149-59. It is also worth considering C. Edwards, 'Translating Empire? Macaulay's Rome' in C. Edwards (ed.), *Roman Presences: Receptions of Rome in European Culture, 1789-1945* (Cambridge University Press, 1999); and in more general terms N. Vance, *The Victorians and Ancient Rome* (Blackwell, Oxford, 1997).

Places to visit

This section can only provide the briefest of overviews of an area of England which is extremely well stocked with Roman remains. Simply driving west from Newcastle along the B6318, following the line of the wall, will reveal a plethora of well-signposted sites and museums, together with a multitude of fascinating little nooks and crannies. Rather than providing an authoritative guide to places which should be visited, this is a list of personal favourites. Those looking for a more extensive and comprehensive list of sites might consider reading chapter 8 of R.J.A. Wilson's *A Guide to the Roman Remains in Britain* (Constable Guide Series, 1988, third edition), or perhaps G. de la Bédoyère's *Hadrian's Wall: History and Guide* (Tempus, 1999).

Birdoswald. This fort can be a little difficult to find (it's just off the B6318, but don't expect signs until you're within two miles) but it's well worth the effort. There's a small museum, which includes a replica of a Roman latrine which can be sat on, and the fort's walls and gates are well-preserved. Little of the interior of the fort is on display, but the two granaries are well laid out: wooden posts marking the dimensions of the fifth-century timber halls are a nice touch. This is a lovely spot to stop and have a picnic, and benches are provided for the purpose. Parents of small children should note that there's an awful lot of space within the fort in which to run about and let off steam; beware, however, the steep drop a short way beyond the southern gateway. As the free leaflet points out, there's a great view from here, and plenty of opportunity to spot wildlife (buzzards, deer, badgers, red squirrels and so on), but it's a long fall into the valley below! Anyone wishing to visit a mile castle can walk a third of a mile out of the east gate to the well-preserved Harrow's Scar Milecastle. For a longer walk, follow the same track past Harrow's Scar and it will lead you to Poltross Burn Milecastle, the abutments of the Roman bridge at Willowford and finally the village of Gilsland (approximately two miles).

Carlisle. There are no sites to be visited in Carlisle, but the Tullie House Museum is extremely good. It contains numerous finds from not only Carlisle but the entire wall, which are generally well presented. Visitors can also walk along a reconstruction of Hadrian's Wall, and fire model catapults.

Carrawburgh. There is a fort here, visible only as a series of grassy banks, but the real attraction must be the Mithraeum, which lies on the other side of the fort from the car park. Entrance is free, and, since it lies right beside the road, it makes an ideal stopping point for those going from Newcastle in search of Housesteads and Vindolanda.

Carvoran. Those particularly interested in the history of the Roman army might consider visiting the Roman Army Museum here, run by the Vindolanda Trust. Its small cinema offers regular showings of a film that gives a guided tour of this section of the wall.

Chesters. This is another lovely site, and thus another great place to stop and have a picnic. A small museum houses the extensive Clayton Collection of Roman sculptures and inscriptions, first begun by Nathaniel Clayton in the early nineteenth-century and continued by his son John. There are some wonderful pieces here, although they would benefit from more careful arrangement and explanation. The site itself is, at first glance, a little disorientating, since Clayton's decision to flatten the site means that the fort walls no longer stand. All four of the gates, however, have been exposed and laid out – together with several of the tower foundations – so that a short walk quickly gives a sense of the dimensions of the fort. The barracks area is particularly well presented, as are the headquarters building and the commander's house (complete with a private bathhouse); it is even possible to walk down a short flight of steps into the underground strong-room, below the headquarters building, in which money and valuables were kept. Just beyond the fort, alongside the river, are the remains of the fort's baths, which are very well explained on a series of signs. It is also possible, when the river is low, to see the abutments of the Roman bridge; the best preserved of these actually lies on the bank on the far side of the river and can be reached from the modern road bridge (this is not part of the Chesters fort site and is thus free). While the river-bank close to the bathhouse is a pleasant place to sit in the sunshine, beware the deep water.

Corbridge. The museum here is excellent, containing a number of carefully explained artefacts of both military and civilian provenance; look especially for the collection of surprisingly modern-looking medical instruments and the beautifully made jewellery. The profusion of walls and pavements at the site itself can, at first, be a little confusing, but well-written signs enable one to get a sense of the remains. Of particular interest are the well-preserved granaries, the remains of the fountain house alongside the granaries, and the aqueduct (more akin to a wide gutter than to the grand structures which march alongside the Appian way outside Rome).

Housesteads. This is perhaps the best presented of the forts of Hadrian's Wall itself. The visitor parks at the visitor centre by the road, before climbing the hill above to Housesteads fort. Tickets for the fort itself can be purchased in the small but interesting museum. The remains of the fort are clearly laid out: the fort's latrine is particularly well preserved. The elderly and disabled who might be put off visiting the site because of the walk should ask in the National Trust Visitors' Centre beside the car park; if the small car park at the top of the hill is empty it may be possible for them to drive to the fort.

Those wishing to walk a little of the wall are advised to turn west from Housesteads fort and amble five miles or so to the Steel Rigg crossroads. For the hardy, a path lies along the wall itself: it undulates significantly, but the views from the top of the hills make it worthwhile. For the less energetic, there is a lower, flatter path (which also allows the walker to traverse a loop). Milecastle 37 lies not far along this stretch of the wall and provides a good example of such a structure. Perhaps a mile west of Housesteads, film buffs may recognise a tree in a dip between two hills: in *Robin Hood, Prince of Thieves* Kevin Costner lands in England, and then promptly finds himself on this spot. For those not feeling at all energetic, this is also visible from the road.

Vindolanda. This is a well-presented site, undergoing constant re-assessment as archaeological investigation progresses. At present, visitors are able to see the fort's water supply, the remains of a Romano-Celtic temple, remains of part of the *vicus*, the military bathhouse, the third century fort, and a modern mock-up of a stretch of Hadrian's Wall itself (accompanied by a model ballista). A short walk down the hill below lies the site museum, the displays of which change to reflect the latest finds from the site. The museum is set in attractive gardens which contain copies of a number of the best-known inscriptions found at Vindolanda (translated on nearby signs), together with detailed and accurate replicas of a house, shop, and temple from the *vicus*. An added attraction during the summer months is the opportunity to watch archaeologists at work excavating parts of the site, and the site is well signed and explained. This site is particularly good for children and includes a cafe.

Wallsend. Situated in Newcastle itself, this site is easily reached using the Metro train system, lying as it does very close to the Wallsend Metro station. The fort is well laid out, and the modern museum is extremely good. It includes a tower from which the site may be viewed, and a thoughtfully presented children's section in which Roman feasts can be planned, Roman games played, and mosaics put together (experience with a group of undergraduates suggests that the children's area may also prove of interest to older age groups). Also on the site is a full reconstruction of a Roman bathhouse.

Index/Glossary